B

of

Love

To Dora
Love
Christopher

Christopher Titmuss

www.insightmeditation.org

Contents

Acknowledgements

I wish to thank various Buddhist centres, organisations and networks, as well as countless people around the world, who kindly invite me to give Dharma teachings. There is no greater privilege than to serve the Dharma.

I have been a small servant of the Dharma in the West since 1976. I have worked on four continents with many thousands of people offering hundreds and hundreds of residential retreats, courses and various programmes, as well as facilitating countless workshops, public talks, dialogues and attending thousands of organisational committee meetings.

Readers will see the influence of countless sessions of reflection, discussion and one to one enquiry in the pages of this book.

As Dharma teachers, we are practitioners who share our understanding. Knowing our strengths and weaknesses, we always have much to learn, to explore and realise. We belong to the first generations of men and women bringing the Dharma wisdom and practices to the West.

I wish to express immense appreciation to the Buddha, Dharma and Sangha, my teachers, Venerable Ajahn Dhammadharo (1914 – 2005), and Venerable Ajahn Buddhadasa (1907 - 1993) of Thailand.

I wish to thank Alexander Von Gontard for editing and his numerous helpful advisory notes. Jenny Wilks kindly examined an initial draft of a number of chapters. Special thanks to Gesine Belser and also to Anne Ashton for final editing of the manuscript.

I have extensively drawn upon transcriptions of my various recorded Dharma talks given worldwide since the 1970's, as well as notes, reflections and on line articles. These notes and transcriptions formed the initial base for several of the essays in this book. An earlier version of a couple of essay appeared on my weekly Dharma blog. Every essay begins with a quote of the Buddha. Poems are drawn from my book of poetry *Poems from the Edge of Time.*

Christopher Titmuss

Introduction

The Buddha of Love points to the significance of love from a spiritual and religious perspective. There is something genuinely spiritual about the variety of expressions of love in daily life. This book serves to remind us of love as a sacred element to be known in family dynamics, romantic relationships, sexuality, generosity, friendships and compassion. We can draw from the first hand experiences and teachings on love as a confirmation of the liberated heart from such major religious luminaries as Jesus and the Buddha. We can explore ways to apply their experiences and teachings to particular circumstances. Contemporary psychology, mystical experiences and changes in consciousness also make an important contribution to revealing the deep importance of love as a spiritual force. *The Buddha of Love* makes a contribution towards placing love firmly in the heart of consciousness.

The spiritual denotes a quality about a human being not restricted to secular values of personal status and personal wealth. A person with a deep sense of the spiritual expresses frequent acts of kindness, the capacity to endure blame and the absence of demands upon others. Spiritual development shows itself in freedom from the need to perpetuate harmful thoughts, words or actions. This loving approach to life confirms the spiritual dimension of a person. Such a person recognises and acknowledges their limits and their failings, while remaining fully committed to the transformation of those patterns and any other forms of behaviour that restrict love.

Love matters. Love really matters. By virtue of our nature, we have the capacity to penetrate to the deepest levels of love and to know a divine life, as well as appreciating the limitless nature of love benefitting countless numbers of people and other expressions of life. The deep questions of life include the human experience of transformative love and its power to manifest itself in every expression of daily life. Such love requires not only an intimacy with love at the feeling level but the capacity to articulate love, express it and, most of all, share it regardless of the consequences.

We can appreciate its various manifestations through the arts, ethics, insights, meditative concentration, mindfulness, values, service, liberation and awakening. We are at our very best when we have the capacity to love without fear, without inhibition, without limits.

A fully valid life endorses, on a daily basis, the exploration of love through the countless number of circumstances that impact upon our lives, and sometimes beset our lives. A truly authentic confirmation of spirituality, love emerges from the deep within into heart/mind/speech/body as a receptive presence whether showing as the small gesture of kindness, the forgiving word or a dedicated life: selfless, transparent and utterly committed to the happiness, welfare and liberation of others. It all counts in small and great matters.

The Buddha remained an undying advocate of the importance of love (*metta*) elevating human beings to a divine status when they abide in love *(Brahma Vihara)*. He refused to set any limits on love offering precious teachings on sending love in all the directions, including towards those of violence who would "tear limb from limb" from our being. He spoke regularly of liberation through love. He spoke of the benefits of love in community, in personal relationships and towards the three kinds of people: friends, strangers and the unfriendly. He reminded the followers of the Dharma of the importance of love in terms of caring for the Sangha of

Dharma practitioners. He spoke of love with regard to our important relationships: parents, family members, teachers, partners and friends. He advocated respect for the teachings, (the Dharma) referring to appreciative joy and gratitude as further expressions of abiding in the Divine.

It is all too easy to confuse acts of love with vested self-interest. The Buddha knew this from personal experience having been brought up in a dysfunctional family. This was due to a controlling and obsessive father, who imposed terrible restrictions on Prince Gautama in the name of paternal love. The Buddha realised that love requires knowledge and understanding of our selves and others.

Supporting the religious norm of his time the Buddha advocated a homeless, nomadic way of life with the emphasis on solitude and on periods with the Sangha (namely the company of wise and fellow practitioners). Shaped to a degree by his time and culture, the Buddha did not see romantic love and sexual intimacy as spiritual practice. He did not see that the act of making love belonged to the fulfilment of the path as well. He sincerely believed that the fully awakened ones had lost all interest in the sexual experience as he believed that sexual activity had to involve unresolved desire: he believed that a fully awakened one had lost all desire to make love.

The act of making love confirms a great happiness. It is a pity that religious leaders, including the Buddha, have emphasised the transcendence of making love. There is a joy in the making of love and the happiness and togetherness that it offers two people. Such intimacy can truly nourish the spiritual life.

Infinite Intimacies and Infinite Distances

Every chapter in this book addresses a particular aspect of love with regular quotes from the words of the Buddha. There is regular reference to the significance of romantic love and sexuality in several chapters, as this aspect of love is generally neglected in the Buddhist tradition and in religion in general. I believe that each chapter stands on its own two feet with a gentle flow on from one chapter to the next. I have drawn extensively from my experiences of working with people, in an out of retreats, on their issues around love, as well as my own experiences over the years. I have also drawn upon my Dharma practice, observations and reflections as a social critic.

It is not an easy balance to draw extensively from the wisdom teachings of the Buddha, acknowledge their limitations and be equally respectful to the realities of the present in Western life. It is the responsibility of the Dharma teacher to integrate the wisdom of the past with the consciousness of the present for the awakening of the Western mind-set. If love breaks all boundaries then we do not have to institutionalise love through religion, marriage or ordination as celibates, unless it is a step that we enjoy exploring. We practice seeing change in as many moments as possible so that we do not demand upon ourselves a single lifelong membership of a faith, a lifelong marriage or a single, lifelong ordination. Our feelings, views and attitudes can evolve and change in the passage of time. Love has the capacity to stay steady despite changes, including major upheavals, welcome or unwelcome, in our daily life.

The exploration of love, in its various faces, must acknowledge the infinite intimacies between each other and equally the infinite distances as well. We have to learn to live with both; we live our solitude and we live our togetherness.

We cannot live a rich and fulfilled life without love of solitude and without love of intimacy with others. We appreciate our solitude and respect the solitude of others as one expression of true companionship. We make ourselves available to be in the company of others and be available for others to be in our company. The Buddha advocated this principle of love of aloneness and love of togetherness, time and time again. We can develop such love through practice and exploration.

I cannot think of anything more challenging than to love another through 'thick and thin'. We have to be willing to make sacrifices, to stand firm in aloneness, to treat the kind words and the spiteful attacks of another with a divine equanimity (to quote the Buddha). We have to take risks with love as it may lead into dissent, disorder and disillusionment, not because of the love, that's not possible, but owing to the shadows of desire, neediness and demands that plague human existence.

We need the ability to reflect on what makes us happy in the sharing and offerings of love and inquire into what makes us unhappy in order to be able to dissolve that unhappiness deep within. The manifestation of any specific kind of love has the capacity to release from the deep within an intensity of happiness, well-being and focussed vision where the love bridges every divide that the mind can imagine. This kind of love has no regard for institutional criteria, social norms, and cultural customs that can inhibit love as much as confirm it. The mindful ones take notice of the conventions but only as considerations, since love remains the overwhelming priority serving as an underlying principle in our daily life.

Stay True to Love.

Love
Christopher Titmuss
Totnes, Devon, England

Chapter One

The Buddha and his Dysfunctional Family

Just because a man is called "Sir,"
it does not mean he is free from habits and clinging. (Sn.620)

King Suddhodhana and Queen Mahamaya of Sakya engaged in the preparation of the birth of their child due to be born in the land of Koliya, east of the Sakyan kingdom of north India. While en route with her entourage, guards and servants to Koliya (the small kingdom of the Queen's birth), Queen Mahamaya suddenly went into labour and gave birth to a baby boy under a sal tree in full blossom in the park in Lumbini on the full moon of May of 563 BC. Born into the warrior caste, Gautama had the duty to follow in his father's footsteps and become the future king as well as enforce the military, political and religious institutions of the nation state.

His mother died seven days after his birth. She lived long enough to see her son's skin with 'a golden hue and his blue eyes like the flax plant.' The Queen's younger sister, Pajapati, took responsibility for bringing up the week-old baby and his privileged upbringing in the royal household ensured isolation from the vicissitudes of the citizens of the Sakyan people.

This, at least, is the legendary account, familiar to most Buddhists. It is difficult to distinguish any historical facts of the life of Gautama, from his birth to his death, from the additional embroidery of some 2600 years of commentary on his life and teachings. Whether factual or embroidered, or probably both, facts matter little in the Indian tradition. Insights may emerge from history or mythology, thus making allowances for embellishment to make a point. The story of

1

the Buddha's life has the potential to shed light on our lives and the all too common dynamic of the dysfunctional family.

Various commonly held incidents in various Buddhist texts and legends indicate the positive and negative aspects of the Buddha's upbringing. From a contemporary analysis, Gautama experienced a dysfunctional family that had repercussions for many years, before and after his awakening under the tree of awakening (bodhi) in Bodh Gaya at the age of 35. Prince Gautama could claim to be a victim of a dysfunctional family but he contributed to it when he fled in the middle of the night from his wife, Yashodhara, his week old son, Rahula, his step mother, his ageing father and other members of his family.

Gautama may not have realised at the time, the long term significance in relationship to women of apparently major and minor events in his life up until the age of 29 years when he ran away. The loss of his mother a few days after his birth must surely have had an impact. Perhaps Gautama did not have total confidence in his step mother when she wanted to join his nomadic Sangha after his awakening? Perhaps he had a general lack of confidence in the ability of women to live the homeless life? He may have felt that it was too radical a step to endorse a Sangha of women wanderers who could be vulnerable on the road, or that a mixed Sangha would lead to suspicion among the laypeople.

Astrologers and clairvoyants predicted that Gautama would become either a great emperor or a buddha. They said that the boy displayed signs in his behaviour of a young man destined for future greatness. While the King felt proud of such predictions by the leading fortune tellers of the time, he also felt intense anxiety that his son would flee the Palace and go on a spiritual search until his became a buddha, a fully enlightened one. The King's fears of losing his successor lead him to exercise an unhealthy control over the upbringing of his son. Unwittingly, his father ruled over a dysfunctional family which impacted on his son, his daughter-in-law, his grandson, his wife, his nephew and the entire royal household.

The story of Gautama's upbringing reminds all of us that the problems of the dysfunctional family go far back in human history. Such issues do not just belong to the malaise of contemporary society.

I met with a 29 year old corporate lawyer for a multi-national oil company. He told me that his father had placed on him years of pressure at home and throughout his education to make a 'real success' of his life. For his father it meant that his son should climb the corporate ladder and by the age of 50, he could be the CEO for the oil company.

"I felt I was living my life to please my father," he told me. "I needed to get out of the oil business and experience the real world. I quit the job. My father was furious. I travelled to India and started living in the real world. My father thinks that I have thrown my life away. Fortunately, my mother, who divorced my father, understands my interest in spiritual matters, compassion and travelling on a small budget."

Like Gautama, we may have to break away from parents who imagine they always know what is best for us. We may have to find our own way in the world. Well-intentioned parents may not realise that their expectations on their children can actually inhibit their growth and development as adults. King Suddhodhana thought he knew what was best for his son. His pressure to get his own way brought about a backlash. The same situation keeps repeating itself in human history.

A Fateful Decision

The King took the fateful decision that his son must lead the most sheltered of existences through hiding him from him the pain facing human beings, such as sickness, ageing and death. Perhaps the King felt his son suffered over the death of his mother days after giving birth to Gautama. He wanted to protect his son from further suffering. Perhaps he believed that his son would then have no need to question life, no need to leave the Royal Family to search for an authentic reality. Gautama thus lived in a world apparently happy, secure, and exposed to the arts, religious learning, sports and intellectual development. Owing to his fears and anxieties, the King gave his son an utterly distorted picture of reality that Gautama eventually rebelled against. The King's worst nightmare eventually came true.

Devadatta, a cousin of the Buddha, proved to be another influential family member whose personal problems contributed to a dysfunctional influence through a lack of empathy with humans, animals and birds. As young boys of similar age, Gautama accompanied Devadatta, who loved hunting. Spotting a beautiful white swan flying overhead, Devadatta took his bow and arrow, aimed and shot the bird through the neck. Gautama ran over to the swan, drew the arrow out and provided a tourniquet to stop the bleeding. Devadatta argued that since he shot the bird he should keep it. Gautama adopted a different viewpoint that since he saved the life of the bird, the fate of the swan rested with him.

Two wise men of the kingdom decreed that those who preserved life had the right to make the claim for its continued support, rather than those whose motivation was to destroy life. In later years, especially after his full awakening, the Buddha consistently gave teachings on compassion which he described as a divine abiding (*Brahma*

4

Vihara) or the kingdom of God in monotheistic language. The incident with Devadatta may have had a significant future influence on Gautama, since after his awakening he consistently advocated the importance of compassion and concern for the welfare of all creatures.

King Suddhodhana invited numerous beautiful young women to his palace so that his son Gautama could select a bride. The young man's eye fell on Yashodhara, whom he subsequently married and the couple moved into the palace, as custom dictated and still does. In the Indian tradition the bride uses her powers of seduction and erotic sexuality to keep the attention of her husband, as the son can find himself living under the demands of his mother and father at the expense of intimacy with his wife.

After his marriage, Gautama personally witnessed the painful signs of human existence: ageing, sickness and death. He also witnessed a yogi on a spiritual search. It is said that King Suddhodhana lived in such fear of his son going on a spiritual quest that he did not allow family, friends or servants to even talk about such suffering in front of the Prince. Despite all the King's efforts, Gautama saw, for the first time, human suffering when Channa, his faithful charioteer, took him on a ride through the capital. He came face to face with human reality, including a corpse, and Channa whispered to him "Everybody will die one day. There is no escape from death."

Gautama clearly felt distress at the sight of individuals who were sick and diseased, decrepit with age, and he was distressed at the sight of a lifeless body. He probably became angry with his father and family for conspiring together to keep him isolated from the real world through his confinement to the Royal Palace and Gardens of Kapilavashtu, the Capital of the Sakyan kingdom. Secrecy and denial eat away at the emotional fabric of the inner life, when

5

members of a family make every effort to hide the Truth as a means of control over another. The evidence shows that Gautama became disillusioned to the point of rejection of everything he had been brought up to believe. Rather than rejoice at the birth of his son, Gautama exclaimed 'bondage' and then named the baby 'Rahula, 'which means bondage.

The obsessively protective and controlling King caused widespread pain and confusion throughout the family living in the palace, while Gautama entered into a personal crisis. Despite the loss of his mother soon after birth, the conflict with Devadatta, a controlling father with family and friends conspiring to hide reality from him, he, nevertheless, had an experience in his youth that made him a lifelong advocate of the power of meditation.

Once a year his father, in his role as King, initiated a ceremony to begin the rice ploughing season. Around the age of 11 or 12 years, Gautama sat in the cross-legged posture in the shade of an apple tree watching the ceremony. While sitting there, the boy effortlessly entered into a deep meditation experiencing happiness, concentration, a glow throughout his cells and inner peace. Gautama recalled this experience, years later, while sitting under the Bodhi tree. He then turned away from severe spiritual austerities and life denying practices towards similar meditative absorptions experienced under the apple tree as a means for a total waking up. In his teachings, he made frequent reference to the power of meditation to know inner peace, happiness and to see into the depths of existence, pleasing and displeasing, welcome and challenging.

Experiences, spiritual, mystical and esoteric, can have a beneficial influence on our daily life. There is a tendency for some people to have such experiences and then move quickly on from them without giving time to digest the significance of the experience. We can forget important moments in our life or push them away as we give more priority to other matters. There is an opportunity to reflect on these experiences to learn something from them. These experiences may point the way to profound realisations and may uncover perceptions of life hidden from us in conventional consciousness. Sitting under the tree, Gautama recalled his meditation experience that had occurred some 23 years earlier. He recalled the inner peace, clarity and happiness that he felt within and realised its potential for a liberating wisdom.

We may need to make time for reflection on any important spiritual experience in our life. Perhaps such an inner event can encourage us to explore further rather than just ignoring it. If our life has been devoid of any spiritual, mystical or esoteric experience, we should engage in some questioning of ourselves. Am I trapped in my five sense and my views about them? Do I believe that true reality depends upon my thoughts about the past, present and future? What steps would I be willing to make to experience an altered state of consciousness?

We do not have to rely upon a spiritual experience to trigger a spiritual quest. The sight of somebody suffering through sickness, the decrepit posture of a very old person and a corpse sparked Gautama's existential search. At the age of 29, he had to face up to the Truths of life free from denial and suppression. Gautama's family had let him down and now he would run away and let them down. A dysfunctional family living in the same household had entered into a crisis.

The Final Straw

The final straw for Gautama came when his father offered a party to celebrate the birth of Rahula, his week old grandson and successor to the throne after Gautama. Musicians, dancers and magicians entertained the numerous guests.

7

Gautama was in no mood for partying. He felt despair with thoughts of future of sickness, pain and death. No one had been honest with him. He had lost faith in them. They had denied him a balanced view of life, and he needed to seek out his own way of life. He resolved to run away and discover for himself what mattered. Even after his awakening he established a *vinaya* (discipline, literally 'to turn away from what is not wholesome'), that strongly discouraged his nomadic Sangha from involvement in entertainment. He wanted them to face up to every aspect of life without denial or avoidance through self-indulgence.

Gautama reacted, in the most direct way possible, to his sheltered upbringing and the pleasures and comforts of a seductive lifestyle. Knowing the emptiness of it, he made up his mind to run away. He would flee from his wife, child and all his responsibilities. Just as his mother had died seven days after the birth of Gautama, Gautama ceased to be a father, both in terms of presence and responsibility by making his escape from the palace seven days after the birth of his son. A strange karma had arisen through this dysfunctional family.

During the night he made his getaway, Gautama felt afraid to take a final look at Rahula and Yashodhara in bed in case he lost his determination and settled for his comfortable and protected lifestyle as a prince, husband and father. Again, years later, after his full awakening under the bodhi tree, Gautama ensured that his teachings and the practices addressed the important issues of daily life. He took a completely different position from his father: instead of trying to establish a pleasurable heaven through a withdrawal from witnessing suffering and sorrow, Gautama advocated the facing up to existence and non-existence: life and death, as it is. It meant bringing mindfulness and awareness, with complete comprehension, to everything whatsoever, no matter how apprehensive or fearful the mind. The Buddha's

8

teachings meant getting close to the 'tiger of suffering', to look into its face and to see clearly that the tiger of terror had no teeth.

The meditation under the apple tree, the compassion for the swan and the human capacity to witness the pain of life formed essential cornerstones of the Buddha's teachings, mattering more than the conventions of family life and following the wishes of parents and other authority figures. The Buddha sanctioned the seeing and knowing of Truth as a higher calling rather than obedience to roles as a married man and father of a child.

Contemporary psychology recognises the impact of childhood influences whether an early bereavement, meditative states, acts of compassion as well as the impact of influential family members in the short and long term. With his capacity for recollection, the Buddha drew extensively from the experiences of his upbringing. He would have sensed the power of his early life as a resource for his awakening and priorities in teaching. Rather than portray himself as a victim of his dysfunctional family, he drew upon his formative years for insights. His story has been a source of inspiration for centuries and has become one of the most famous stories in human history.

The life story of the Buddha shows the heart and mind of a man who has not rejected the past, nor denied its influence, but he has positively acknowledged influential and informative experiences. His awakening shed light on various experiences so that he understood clearly their causation, rather than acting as a shadow or an obscuration of a liberated life. We also have the capacity, if necessary, to track our childhood influences upon our adult life so that we have the capacity to recognise those experiences that provide insight to develop what is healthy, and the ability to let go and dissolve what is unhealthy.

Owing to his vested self-interest in his son becoming his successor, King Suddhodhana extended so much control over freedom of speech on his family that Gautama reacted aggressively and he could not offer his presence to his new born son. There has been a lot of criticism over the centuries of Buddha's decision to avoid responsibility as a father, husband and future King of his country. This long-standing historical viewpoint fails to distinguish the mind-set of a young man obviously experiencing an existential crisis and burdened with the problem of a fixed and programmed life, from his becoming a Buddha at the age of 35. In such a tightly controlled family dynamic, Gautama could not address the core issues of what really matters in the movement between birth and death and possibly beyond.

The mind of Gautama the Prince was utterly different from the awakened mind of Gautama the Buddha. Gautama makes this distinction between the pre-awakening consciousness and the post awakening consciousness. To put it in simple terms, the Buddha did not run away from the comforts of the Palace. A disillusioned 29 year old man tormented with doubt and confusion fled the Palace to try to gain some resolution to burning questions about life and death. His quest ended with the discovery of the Deathless while under the Bodhi tree.

There are numerous voices from politicians, the business community and the family who insist on their prescription for a good life, generally meaning personal success through social standing, career, disposable income and acquisition of desirable consumer goods and property. The compelling attraction towards these goals offers a rather narrow view of a fulfilled life. The spiritual quest offers the potential for a different vision of life, nourishing and enlightening. Unlike Gautama, it does not mean that the seeker must flee their personal circumstances, unless one feels trapped and overwhelmed with confusion and despair.

The quest may include the exploration of meaning, purpose, love and the natural inter-connection we have with everybody and everything. The spiritual quest puts materialism and the material world in its perspective enabling consciousness to be receptive to meditation, to the inner world, the natural world and the sense of wonder and inquiry into what it means to be human.

The account of Gautama's spiritual quest continues to resonate with countless numbers of women and men who search to resolve deep issues and questions about life. In that respect, there is a timeless element to his story. A single recollection of an experience in the past or present can become the event that changes the direction of our life forever.

A Return Home

A decade after his awakening, the Buddha finally agreed to the request of his ageing father to make the 600 kilometre walk from Rajghir to Kapilavasthu. The Buddha's first meeting with his father did not go well. When he heard that the Buddha went on alms round begging for food every morning, the imperious King told his son. "The warrior caste never goes on an alms round."

The Buddha replied: "The lineage of the Buddhas have always received alms."

The Buddha showed such little concern for the caste system, royal protocol and family life; he offered instead the alternative of the Sangha family and daily disciplines instead of protocol.

There is a telling incident with regard to the anguish and sorrow felt by Yashodhara upon the Buddha's return to see his family. Instead of happiness and delight, when her

11

attendants spotted the Buddha walking towards the walls of the city, she sent her son, Rahula, to meet him.

Yashodhara had experienced not only a betrayal but bereavement at the loss of Gautama. This left her husband's father taking on the role of the father to Rahula, his grandson. It is said in the tradition that Yashodhara said to her son: "Do you know who that is?" Rahula replied: "That's the Buddha, mother." His mother replied: "That's your father." With tears in her eyes, Yashodhara told Rahula to collect his inheritance. "What belonged to the father must be passed on to the son," she told Rahula. The Buddha listened to his son. It is said that the thought arose in the Buddha's mind "My son is asking for his father's wealth but I can offer him an inner wealth that is seven times more precious."

Impressed with his father's way of life, Rahula joined the nomadic Sangha. This brought further anguish to his grandfather, having lost his son and now his grandson. The King probably regretted inviting the Buddha to the palace. The Buddha agreed to the King's request to, in future, seek permission from parents/guardians whenever children decided they wanted to join the wandering Sangha. The Buddha had not applied this guideline with regard to his son. In his anguish, the King sent delegation after delegation to try to win his grandson back.

The Buddha also encouraged his half-brother, Nanda, the son of the King and Queen Pajapati to join his nomadic Sangha. This brought further anguish to the King and Queen and added further distress because Nanda left home on the day of his marriage to the beautiful Janapada. It meant again that the King and Queen had lost another heir to the throne. It was not long before Nanda experienced doubt about leaving behind his beautiful wife. The Buddha told him that the happiness of Nirvana meant much more than the happiness of marriage to a beautiful woman, adding that Nanda would have to find out through his own experience.

The differences between the Buddha and his father around caste and family duty took years to resolve and led to a major inner transformation for his father. Gautama attended his father's funeral.

Queen Pajapati pleaded with the Buddha to allow her to join the Sangha after the death of her husband. The Buddha refused to give her the opportunity to make the transition from home to homelessness. He gave no explanation for refusing his stepmother. It became another indication of yet another rift in the family. Later both the Queen and her daughter-in-law, Yashodhara, approached Ananda (the Buddha's first cousin), for support to join the Sangha.

Ananda, who acted as personal attendant to the Buddha, asked the Buddha a direct question: "Are women equally capable of achieving full awakening?" The Buddha agreed that women had the same potential for full awakening (to become a Buddha). The Buddha then had to let go of any misgivings about his stepmother and his wife renouncing their privileged life to become Dharma practitioners. Once he opened the door to the two women, he made it possible for all women to leave the 'dusty life of the householder' and join his wandering network, free from the social/religious constraints imposed upon women. Thus he facilitated the first liberation movement for women who were denied the same choice as men.

Buddhist texts claim the Buddha demanded that an ordained woman, even if ordained for many, many years, must bow first to a monk who had been ordained for only one day. Another rule prohibited nuns from reproving monks in any way, but monks were allowed to reprove nuns. There is a strong suspicion that conservative monks, long after the death of the Buddha, added such extra rules for men and women in order for men to maintain control over the Sangha.

The Buddha seemed determined to develop a rather austere tradition, even if it meant rejecting kind offers from members of the royal family and other wealthy supporters. Queen Pajapati offered the homeless Sangha finely woven cloth to wear. The Buddha refused such fine material as he felt it could have a corrupting impact on their simple way of life. His step mother would not have found it easy to hear his good intentions from her stepson.

The difficult family dynamics may have been a factor influencing the mind of the Buddha when he showed such resistance to the request of his stepmother to join the order of practitioners. Three times he refused his stepmother's request to join the Sangha. It is not easy to apply the fusion of family and spiritual life with the interpersonal dynamics affecting all those concerned.

It was never easy for the Buddha dealing with a family constellation where the shadows of roles: such as husband, wife, son, father, grandfather, stepmother, cousin, half-sister and half-brother, wanted to engage with the Buddha and his rapidly expanding spiritual movement. Wise and emotionally well integrated family members have the responsibility to explore ways to resolve family disputes and sometimes take tough decisions. Sometimes the creator of a project may have to say "no" to family involvement, even though it hurts the feelings of close relatives and loved ones.

Wise counsel of others outside of the family matters a great deal in terms of making a contribution towards establishing a genuine sense of harmony and well-being between relatives and loved ones. Sometimes one family member knows that he or she cannot communicate with another, no matter how wise and compassionate the person, such as the Buddha. The voice of wise counsel may carry more weight, be more effective and healing than close family members trying to sort out all of their own problems. For example, the Buddha's stepmother and wife went to Ananda to seek support to join the Sangha as the Buddha had blocked their way.

We may have the blessing of loving and dedicated parents who wish to be involved in our initiatives or projects. They may offer all kinds of support, such as time, money and presence, but we sense that we could be storing up trouble in the future. Family members might find themselves engaging in squabbles, if not conflict, over disagreements in the decision making process. An intensity of tension and disputes can arise between parents and children with parents thinking they know best because of their seniority.

Yet flexibility matters, rather than holding to an intransigent attitude. The Buddha listened to Ananda, his personal attendant, who reminded him men and women equally have the opportunity for a liberated life. The situation of the Buddha serves as a reminder that we may need to listen to the counsel of good friends when expressing a standpoint about members of our family. Friends may see a different angle on the family dynamics.

Support for Members of the Family

The Buddha permitted men, women and children in his family to explore the Dharma of ethics, meditation, wisdom and the disciplines of an austere lifestyle. It was not always easy for family members to make the shift from their identity as members of a family to one of Dharma student with a family member, Gautama, as their Dharma teacher. Though Gautama fled his family and responsibilities for six years, he, nevertheless, supported, albeit reluctantly at first, the daily presence of his family, as well as being an active role model to his son in daily life.

Sundari-Nanda, daughter of King Suddhodhana and Queen Pajapati and half-sister of the Buddha, came to be regarded as the most beautiful woman in Sakya. When she joined the Sangha the Buddha reminded her that parts of the body were not beautiful but were subjected to ageing, wrinkles, sickness, disease and decay. She said: *"I practise to perceive the body fully. I looked at it this way night and day. I am now carefree, quenched, calm and free."*

At first glance, it might appear that the troublesome family dynamic that had gone on for years, had been finally resolved through the noble motivations and intentions of all concerned. It was far from being the case. The Buddha's cousin, Devadatta, also joined the Sangha under the influence of unresolved personal shadows: power seeking, jealousy and an underlying hatred of the Buddha's success and inspiration that he offered many, including members of his own family. Devadatta tried to organise a spiritual coup to depose the Buddha and replace himself as the leader of the Sangha. His vitriolic hatred of the Buddha reached such an intensity that Devadatta attempted to assassinate Gautama on three occasions: by getting an elephant to charge down on the Buddha to trample him to death, by throwing a boulder from a ledge, and by paying hired killers (who had a change of heart after listening to the Buddha).

It is not unusual, in any extended family, for an individual to carry the shadows of other family members as well as their own shadows. One family members absorbs backbiting, fault-finding and blame from other members of the family which only intensifies their unresolved rage. When the self feels unloved and unwanted, it usually pursues attention seeking activities to get away from lack of self-worth. Devadatta sought to create a division in the Sangha

16

through the introduction of additional disciplines as a means to generate the sense of self importance, and to overcome the lack of self-worth. Devadatta wanted the Sangha to become vegetarian as he knew the Buddha took a tolerant view of meat eating, provided animals were not specifically killed for his Sangha. Gautama considered it more important to examine what comes out of our mouths in terms of what we say, rather than what goes in. A Buddha today would surely advocate a vegetarian diet out of compassion for animals, birds and fish, for health reasons and wise use of land and food resources; though perhaps not impose it as a hard and fast rule in the way that Devadatta demanded.

At the time of the Buddha, and right up until today, yogis, wandering mendicants, spiritual seekers and similar networks of people who depend on householders for their daily meal, would live naturally as vegetarians. It is virtually unheard of in India to feed meat and fish to yogis. The refusal of the Buddha to endorse a vegetarian diet meant that few Buddhist monks and nuns today live as vegetarians. In fact, some monks and nuns today eat more meat and fish than householders because laypeople like to offer them such food since it is the most expensive food to buy. Householders believe they make more merit in offering meat and fish.

Many Buddhists have religious sensitivities and hesitate to become vegetarians because it could appear they are taking sides with Devadatta. It is believed that Devadatta eventually persuaded some 500 followers (500 is a metaphorical term and in the texts means 'a lot' to leave the Sangha and to follow him when he had formed a cult to act in competition with the Buddha's Sangha.

The Buddha surely knew the mind of his cousin. He had had the painful interaction with him over the swan when both men were boys. He would have heard about the hostility and jealousy of his cousin towards himself.

17

Today, a family can undergo an intensity of differences involving beliefs, values, money and interpretation of events. In the intensity of family dynamics, we have to find ways to stay true to ethical principles even though major risks might be the outcome. It would surely not have been easy to invite his stepmother, stepbrother, wife and son to an austere way of life, where their entire possessions in the Sangha could rest on an outstretched arm and with servants and officials agreeing to their every whim.

Out of compassion, the Buddha eventually agreed to members of the family joining his Sangha while knowing that difficult issues would arise. In a one to one talk with his son, the Buddha emphasised the importance of Truthfulness in speech (perhaps an echo of his pain due to his father's deceit about the realities of life). The Buddha's teachings make it clear that we learn to take responsibility for the condition of our inner life. We do not need to live in blame and fault finding of others, including parents and other important family members, no matter how dysfunctional the family.

Our First Gods

The Buddha described our parents as our first gods when, as children, we revere them. He went on to say that our parents are also our first teachers and worthy of donations (*dana*) as our parents introduced us into this world, cared for us and nourished us. As adults, we show our respect to them through honouring what they have done for us and giving them gifts such as food, drink, clothing and bedding. He said a son or daughter supports his parents through:

- *engaging in tasks for them,*
- *supporting the tradition of the family,*

18

- *living a worthy life,*
- *giving dana on their behalf when they die,*
- *living without causing harm to others.*

Parents act in sympathy with their sons and daughters by:
- *restraining them from unhealthy behaviour,*
- *exhorting virtue, values and ethics,*
- *training them for a profession,*
- *contracting a suitable marriage*
- *and in due time handing over their inheritance. (D.III.189)*

The Buddha gave reminders to parents and their children of matters that deserve mindfulness and reflection so that the whole family lives in 'mutual accord' with each other. He also had his responsibilities as father with regard to his son who he neglected for the first six years of the boy's life. The Pali suttas (the texts recording the Buddha's discourses) include the essence of some of the conversations the Buddha had with his son.

"What do you think, Rahula: What is a mirror for?"
"For reflection," Rahula replied.
"In the same way, Rahula, bodily actions, verbal actions, & and mental actions are to be done with repeated reflection:
"If on reflection, you know that your actions would not cause affliction, then it is fit for you to do. If, on reflection, you know that it is not causing suffering, you may continue with it. He said to his son: "If, on reflection, you know that it led to self-affliction, to the affliction of others, or to both; then you should confess it, reveal it, lay it open to the teacher or to a knowledgeable companion. You should exercise restraint in the future." MLD 61.

The same principle again applied to speech and mind. The Buddha advocated that his son share his experiences rather than suppress them. The Buddha knew the significance of listening/counselling/ to resolve unresolved problems involving actions of body, speech or mind that led to painful consequences.

The Buddha promoted *"skilful actions with pleasant consequences are fit to do."*

"Rahula, all priests and meditators in the past, present and future who dwelt in purity (absence of greed, negativity and ignorance) *did so through repeated reflection."*

The Buddha concluded: *"That's how you should train yourself."* Rahula told his father he was delighted with the advice he received from his father. (MLD 61)

The dialogue between the Buddha and his son shows the love and trust between man and boy. This trust develops through years of daily acts from the father through his presence, his loving kindness and the capacity to recognise the son's needs. Children need to know when parents give advice that their parents 'walk the talk,' especially when parents give blunt advice to their children. So when the Buddha spoke of the importance of skilful actions and repeated reflection, Rahula knew his father remained committed to such a way of life. Instead of resisting the advice of his father, Rahula told him of his delight in listening to such advice.

Skilful action and regular reflection enable us to evolve as human beings. As we practice to walk our talk, it may mean at times that we take three steps forward and one step back. Reflection safeguards us from taking four steps back.

To his nomadic Sangha, the Buddha said:

"I lived a very spoilt life (as a Prince). I saw an old man. All delight in youth left me. I saw a sick person subjected to disease. All delight in health left me. I saw a dead person. All delight in life left me."

From his personal experience of a dysfunctional family life, the Buddha subsequently took a realistic approach to such matters. He gave a simple injunction in response to a problematic upbringing.

"Develop and practice trust if our parents were untrustworthy.
Develop and practice wholesome actions if our parents engaged in unwholesome behaviour.
Develop and practise generosity if our parents were mean."

If we experienced loving parents, he said, then we repay them for their efforts with our inner development. He said: *"If one should carry one's mother on one shoulder and one's father on the other, and while doing so should live a hundred years, even by that one would not do enough for one's parents to repay what they have done for us."* (AN. Chapter of the Twos) These principles of autonomy and the willingness to trust in one's own experience and insights, at the expense of parents and the other gods of influence in our daily life, show a sense of inner worth even if the family constellation becomes somewhat fractured as a result.

At the end of his life, the Buddha declined to make any family member head of the Sangha or appoint one of the liberated ones in the Sangha as head. The Buddha told Ananda to tell the Sangha to make the Dharma their teacher.

Conflicts

Legend says that King Suddhodhana and King Pasenadi (of the neighbouring Kosala kingdom) were in constant conflict. The King of the Kosalas wanted to marry one of the Sakyan princesses but King Suddhodhana deceived the Kosala King and offered him a beautiful slave. The slave married the King of Kosala and gave birth to a son who found out about the deceit and vowed revenge on the Sakyans. He murdered his father and declared war on the Buddha's homeland. Generals and soldiers believed in a superstition that their army could not invade another country if they met a holy man on the way. The Buddha attempted to stop the war on the Sakyans by sitting under a dead tree. When the Buddha left the tree, the army returned to launch the battle.

Shortly after the death of the Buddha, often referred to as Sakyamuni (the Silent One of the Sakyans), the Kosalans massacred the Sakyan people. It was another tragic consequence to the control, pressure and deceit by King Suddodhana and the devastating impact upon his family and his people.

We can learn about the significance of causation, compassion and wisdom, from the dynamics of the Buddha's difficult family history. The Buddha, who used his insights into his upbringing to form part of his teachings, shows that we can draw insights from our family history and apply them to daily life.

We may need to look into the dynamics of several members of our family. Are there family members that we can rely upon? Are there family members who express problematic states of mind? Are there family members who are insecure and vulnerable? Do we have any unresolved issues? What steps can we take? In what ways can different members of the family come together to give support to each other or support a particularly troubled individual?

The Buddha adopted a practical approach that we can summarise today: Mindfulness of thinking, words (speaking/writing) and actions matter. If we know there is kindness or supportive concern in our thoughts, words and actions, then we follow through. If there is negativity or blame, then we mindfully breathe in and out to clear the mind. We reflect on the changes necessary to develop a clear comprehension of situations with a healthy attitude and the necessary insights for the way forward. These are challenging and memorable principle for the benefit of oneself and others as an important contribution to an awakened life

Chapter 2

Romantic Love as the Path to Awakening

*Let none deceive another. Let his or her thoughts
of boundless love pervade. Sn. 148.150*

The story of Gautama the Buddha appears to serve as a poor
role model for romantic love and marriage. He felt trapped.
He had no sense of any path of awakening in his marriage. He
couldn't cope with being the father of his seven day old son,
Rahula. If he and his beautiful wife, Yasodhara, had had the
wisdom and maturity to see marriage as a vehicle for
realizations, he might not have had to flee the palace nor reject
his role as husband and father.

Six years later, he had a profound and liberating
awakening about the nature of Truth. First, he walked from
Bodh Gaya to Sarnath, near Varanasi, where he gave his first
teachings to five friends who followed an intense path as
yogis. To his credit, from there, he walked to Kapilavasthu to
see his wife, Yasodhara, and his six year old son, Rahula. He
shared with them what he had come to understand. Both his
wife and his son then followed his teachings and adopted a
nomadic way of life.

The Buddha spoke primarily to monks and nuns
leading a celibate life but he also met with many people from
every walk of life. His teachings on love, including romantic
love, have a genuine relevance today for finding insight and
wisdom in relationships. He frequently encouraged the
exploration of the depths of love, compassion, appreciative joy
and equanimity, as well as a sustained inquiry into the
conditional sequence going from initial contact to feelings to
desire and clinging, so problematic for people. There are
countless other insights in the Buddha's teachings that shed

24

light on human relationships, e.g. the responsibilities between two people, the importance of clear communication, working with desire, seeing into I, me and mine. To their credit, some couples really apply the teachings to their relationship and share their experiences together. The couples are on the same wavelength. Differences in age, experience, role and background become secondary.

There are numerous views and opinions about romantic love, sometimes based on one's own experiences, sometimes based on the experience of others, or simply drawing conclusions without any real experience. For example, some people suspect that falling in love merely amounts to a positive projection upon another person, even if it leads to a relationship, marriage and children. Some regard falling in love as feelings of infatuation. They regard such expressions of love as a temporary phenomenon until the other person is seen, warts and all. They might even point out that they base their view on first-hand experience.

Many counsellors offer a wise and skilful perception when counselling couples experiencing problems in a relationship. Their voice can contribute to a healing process with the two people recognising how much they share and working to find ways to resolve their differences. A counsellor, a couple, family and friends, sometimes conclude with an alarming degree of self-assurance that 'romantic love won't last.' One couple told me their counsellor said that romantic love fades as the two partners get to know each other in the course of time. One partner or both may react against such a voice of inevitability.

There are no shortages of people who can confirm how transitory romantic love is. Experienced counsellors would surely hesitate to draw such a fateful conclusion: that romantic love is always an initial temporary phase. Others know that romantic love is a love sent from heaven, an opportunity for deep discovery about the nature of love, and has the capacity to stay true and steady throughout a life. Those who dismiss romantic love as merely a positive, transitory projection upon another become blind to its sustainable and transformational power.

Yes, the feelings and experience of romantic love often undergo change, but that fact applies to everything else as well. It is equally true to say of any experience that it will not last. There are no degrees and no exceptions to the transitory nature of events. Romantic love is, no more or less, transitory than anything else. It can rise and fall and rise again within the same relationship. The act of being in love, with the attention linked to another, provides a powerful catalyst for discovery about its power to accommodate differences and change.

The Reciprocation of Love

Once the other person reciprocates with a similar kind of love, then the passions will probably enliven even more. This love loosens all the inner restraints. Like a moth becoming a beautiful butterfly, romantic love belongs to the realm of a divine abiding where the lover feels to be on top of the world. Numerous other concerns drop away. The mutuality of the love serves as a doorway into the divine revealing expressions of creative imagination, but the romantic remains vulnerable to sliding into fantasy and projections that fall flat at a later date. If the glamour of being in love fades away, it can leave a trail of disappointment and the self then wonders what was all that about? The wise lover acknowledges the power of transference and high esteem for the other while, at the same time, is aware of the whole person amidst the archetype embodying an ideal.

The presence of Eros in an encounter challenges every aspect of being. It is one of the most powerful of all human experiences. Being in love can affect our appetite. Our heart beats faster, butterflies fly around in the stomach and words are hard to put together. The intensity of the experience of Eros overwhelms the person's feelings who then find that they have difficulty sleeping at night and cannot stop thinking about the other person. Doubts can arise about the other person's feelings or whether this intense love confirms a delusion. Does beauty lie in the eye of the beholder? Is this real? What is happening to me? I have never felt like this before!

Romantic love shifts consciousness into the divine realms for a heavenly kind of Dharma practice. The heart, thoughts and body cells become stimulated and energised through the act of being in love with another. The lover cannot choose to fall in love with another since it is essentially a movement of the heart, not a rational decision. It can become a transformative experience, with or without any obvious intention. Yet, the mind may need to reflect on the experience of falling in love, the benefits, any concerns and any considerations for the person towards whom the love is directed.

Love has an indispensable place in human life. In the discourse on the *Four Applications of Mindfulness*, the Buddha exhorts us to see the 'feelings in the feelings'. There is a consistent encouragement for us to explore feelings, fully and totally, to attend to them, to listen to them, to acknowledge them, whether pleasant, unpleasant or between the two, and to respond to feelings. In his book 'The Psychology of Transference', Carl Jung told the story of Faust who had a shattering experience when he was taken out of his "deadly dull rut" in his laboratory through realising that 'feeling is all.'

27

The Buddha would concur with the recognition of the importance of feelings for human beings.

Inquiry into Love

For many years, I have taken a deep interest in the nature of romantic love following some moments of inspirational insight involving much learning, through precious and difficult times, along the way. These explorations directed me in fresh ways to explore love and its extraordinary potential for awakening, particularly the force of love called Eros between a man and woman (and, of course, for some through same sex relationships). I meditated, reflected, shared with others, and listened to others on the theme of romantic love as a major feature of exploration and inquiry, both in and out of a personal relationship.

I read books on romantic love and relationships. Some books I pulled off the self-help bookshelves in High street shops or at airports. Friends recommended books to me. I read books by David Deida, John Gray, Stephen Levine, Barry Long and Robert Johnson. I read books on Tantra, Indian Gods and Goddesses, Eros, archetypes, Greek mythology and the history of Western love. It was fascinating reading. Some of the books were insightful; some were very lightweight or riddled with simplistic generalisations.

Worthwhile reading for reflection, inspiration and insight are important features for awakening through romantic love. I found a very well researched book on love, romance, passion, Eros and the way such experiences challenge the deepest places within. I first knew about the book through a small advertisement in the *London Review of Books* magazine.

The Title of the book is:

DREAMS OF LOVE AND FATEFUL ENCOUNTERS

The Power of Romantic Passion
Author: Ethel Spector Person, M.D.
Publisher: American Psychiatric Publishing Inc.
Washington, DC and London, England. 378 pages.

It is intelligent, incisive and reveals a genuine depth of inquiry. Chapter titles include 'Falling in Love', 'How Love Develops', 'Struggles', 'Disillusionment, 'Love and Power', 'Transference' and 'Love that Endures.' I found these themes invaluable. There are quotes from a range of authorities on these and other aspects of intimate love, quotes from other books on the subject, from fiction, from poets and the world of psychology. I learnt much about the love lives of some of our writers and deep thinkers and much about myself. The book addresses the heart and mind with the support of serious academic research. Ethel Person has really looked deeply into matters of love. She has written an illuminating book on a challenging subject – a book to read and read again. I can open it at any page and find some invaluable Truth in it. I find it helpful to read some passages slowly to let the insights go deep. I regard it as an indispensable resource.

We learn about love through the insights and wisdom of others. We learn through errors of judgement and we learn through insights. Jesus, Shakespeare, Rumi, Carl Jung, John Keats act as my major mentors on matters of the heart, on romantic love, fearless love and the power of Eros. We need inspiration, courage, illumination, and wise counsel when in relationship with another. It is an adventure to explore love with another. My opportunity to be in beautiful relationships, along with years of reflection, exploration and reading, show

29

the support that Dharma teachings and practices can support the development of an intimate relationship. The commitment between two people honours and respects the lives of each other. There is a recognition of the intimacy that both share while simultaneously acknowledging the independence of the two people. The outcome of a wise approach to a dedicated relationship reveals itself in ethics, values, love, happiness and a deep sense of peace and trust in each other. The noble ones living with a profound wisdom share and express the same qualities of heart and mind.

Four Kinds of Relationships

Buddhism has neglected the power of romantic love between two people and has preferred to concentrate of developing loving kindness. Yet the Buddha had recognised the importance of such love and its capacity to shift consciousness into the realm of the gods. While sitting in the shade at the foot of a tree and while travelling along the road between Madhura and Veranja, the Buddha entered into a conversation with several couples. The Buddha, a formerly married man himself, said there are four kinds of relationships (AN IV.53).

- *The couple who live a wretched life together – abusive, stingy, self-indulgent and negligent of each other.*
- *The woman's heart is free from abusive and negligent reactions to her partner. The Buddha said in such a situation: "A wretch lives with a goddess."*
- *The man's heart is free from abuse and negligent reactions. "A god lives with a wretch," he said.*
- *The man and woman care deeply for each other with their hearts free of any ill intent or negligence. The*

Buddha concluded that in such a relationship: "A god lives with a goddess."

Religion and secular culture often uphold the view that a relationship works if it continues for a long time, and see it as a failure if it ends. Dharma practice reveals a different view altogether from this conventional one. Two people may embark on a loving and committed relationship, offering each other an opportunity to learn much about themselves and about each other. The dynamics can expose a range of experiences and the potential to realise liberating Truths. The intimacy may last for a few weeks, months, years or even decades. At some point in time, the two people may agree to shift from an intimate relationship, as committed partners, to friendship. One person's Dharma practice may take them in one direction and the partner's practice may lead in another direction. The relationship need not fall apart.

The two people have the wisdom and respect for each other to make such a change. Of course, one or both people may feel some sadness during this transition period into friendship. It is unfortunate that certain people, married or single, can take a condescending view about short relationships. Men and women who have had several relationships at different times over the years, are worthy of support as much as those who stay in a relationship in the long term.

A couple with children, who end their relationship or marriage, can cooperate to ensure that the children feel loved and supported at all times. A wise and loving response matters. Men and women, steady in themselves, also can know a fulfilled life through a network of friendships and love of solitude. For those who maintain a long term relationship, there is no evidence to show that marriage and children offer a

31

more fulfilled life than people who are single and childless. Those who are single and childless can also know a passion for life and experience the romance of life.

A human being has the great potential to live liberated way of life.

The Awakening of Romantic Love

The awakening of romantic love releases a powerful energetic force within. There is no real control over this force. Such love can make a person feel vulnerable through so much concentration of attention on another person. There is the interest in the smallest signal of loves' reciprocation from that man or woman. Something deep and mysterious suddenly recognises something beautiful in another, generating a loving and erotic interest. Thoughts and images reflect the infinite potential of the situation, as the divine within recognises the divine without.

The power of such love raises a question:. Do you love the whole person, as a single, undivided human, or do you love specific qualities of the person, such as kindness, beauty, humour or intelligence? At times, you may have to reflect on whether your love is an undivided love or a love based on qualities. Wisdom supports love for the whole person and also supports love for the qualities of a person. In the passage of time, the person may need to make wise decisions based on their current perceptions. An underlying love has the power to endure.

As a path, romantic love directs the person towards the fullness of consciousness, freeing up from the mundane. Such love can put a person's life into a completely different orbit, releasing opportunities held back through passive routine and the ordinariness of the human realm. Being in love can move consciousness out of the mundane materialistic demands of the mind, giving time to re-evaluate what life is all about. No wonder many people of all ages and temperaments find themselves fascinated and intrigued with a story of romantic love, with its depth, acts of intimacy, and potential to be cast into heaven and hell.

Passion includes the taking of risks with feelings to make this manifestation of love into a path of awakening. Eros can bring out the deepest happiness as well as the intensity of anguish and disappointments. At times, foolishness, impulsive actions and errors of judgement become the raw material for learning and insights. Those who cling to moral absolutes about love, intimacy and sexuality block the opportunity to learn and to grow.

The experience of romantic love engages in a spiritual movement of consciousness, full of incredible potential to find out about the inner life, what we know and do not know about ourselves and equally, what we know and do not know about another. Two people, totally in love with each other, abide as a god and goddess in a divine realm, not of this world. Perhaps more than any other expression of love, romantic love can suddenly catapult two people quickly into the company of the gods. There is the opportunity to reflect, meditate and inquire on the sublime Truths of the heart. Communion reveals a sublime unity.

In the Buddhist tradition, the high status given to a Buddhist monk often leaves the impression that celibacy matters more than passion and sexual intimacy. Some meditators think that when they have developed enough depth, they will no longer be vulnerable to falling in love. They believe their meditation practices will cool all passions for intimacy and they will transcend sexual passion.

It is important to dispute this long standing view perpetuated by far too many yogis, monks and others living a celibate life. This view limits love to the human realm of friendship, simple acts of loving kindness and excludes love expressed through sexual intimacy. That intention to move consciousness out of the reach of romantic love may be a desirable end for some. Solitude, celibacy and personal meditation practice have immense value as long as there is no forming of a view that intimate love is a distraction to Dharma practice. Others, deeply committed to the Dharma, positively welcome the challenge of being in love and the act of making love as a celebration of life. Wisdom shows the mark of an evolved spiritual life, not celibacy.

It is worthwhile to take note of this long-standing religious joke.

A young monk arrives at the monastery to help the other monks in copying the old texts by hand. He notices the monks are copying copies, and not the original books. He points out to the Abbot that if there were an error in the first copy, that error would be continued in all of the other copies. The Abbot says, "We have been copying from the copies for centuries, but you make a good point, my son."

So, the Abbot goes down into the cellar with one of the copies to check it against the original. Hours later, nobody has seen him. So, the young monk goes downstairs to look for him. The young monk finds the Abbot in distress. He asks the Abbot: "What's wrong?"

"We have made a huge mistake. We have misled everybody. The word is celebrate not celibate," says the old monk with tears in his eyes.

I wonder if it is a true story! We have to let go of the mental construct that celibacy is above sexual intimacy. Love matters. We can express it in a variety of ways. The story reminds us that celebration, the expression of appreciative joy, truly belongs to an awakened life. There is an equal real value, too, in celibacy for those who love solitude and friendship without the need for an intimate relationship.

The Transformative Power of Romantic Love

Being in love has certain similarities to the rapture and happiness of the *jhanas* (meditative absorptions) since it can contribute to a wondrous shift of consciousness that naturally subdues the potency of problematic states of mind. Of course, *jhanas* rely on the inner world and being deeply in love relies upon the other. Mindfulness and clear comprehension distinguishes the depth of love from flirtatious behaviour, an ego trip or the pleasure in eliciting such similar feelings from another.

Physical attraction, self-interest, and affectionate attention can produce projections disguised as love. The desire to satisfy personal needs corrupts romantic love. It is all too easy to become infatuated with the desire to get another to fall under the sway of our attention. The exploration of the power of Eros with the Dharma perspective includes integration with ethics. Samadhi (namely a meditative single pointed attention to the beloved), supported with happiness, contributes to heartfelt insights and realisations for both partners.

THE POWER OF EROS

Are we making love without our bodies?
Are we renouncing the fixed form
for the indefinable?
Is this what we share?
It seems so deep that it cannot make sense,
even to ourselves.

What is this middle way that belongs

35

neither to passive friendship,
nor active passion
but a spiritual sensuality
that reveals a sacred centre?

We cannot construct form
out of this formless dimension,
only let our hearts run with the wind,
until we land in the field,
far away from all that we've known before.

Poems from the Edge of Time.

In some situations there is hesitancy, an inner voice of doubt about one's worthiness to speak what one feels. The willingness to let another know of the wish to develop a relationship is never easy. It necessitates venturing out of the safety zone, where caution acts as the reins upon the possibility, for an adventure in love:

- *Are you in pursuit of intensely pleasurable sensations?*
- *Are you in the spell of fantasy?*
- *Are you willing to take risks?*
- *Do you fall in love with alarming frequency?*
- *How do you approach wisely him or her?*
- *Is falling in love to fill an empty space within?*
- *Is there a latent tendency towards attraction?*
- *What is missing in your life?*
- *What do you say to her or him?*

It requires commitment, and deep interest in the heart, to ensure that romantic love and the path of awakening work seamlessly together from the first moment our attention falls upon another. There is often an anxiety, a fear of rejection, and a terror that others will misunderstand. It is not going too far to say that making love is a religion of two. It features various forms of language of love, creative and ritualistic sexual intimacy. As a religious experience, love brings us closer to the deepest place in our heart, closer to another, and bridges any chasm between two people.

Love defies the odds, and has enormous strength. The protests from outsiders, muted or outspoken, often have a similar ring to them. These are typical derogatory reactions:

- *He's looking for a mother figure.*
- *I don't trust her/him one bit.*
- *It won't work out.*
- *S/he is trying to recover her/his lost youth.*
- *S/he needs to be admired.*
- *S/he should leave him/her.*
- *S/he's so materialistic and s/he's so spiritual.*
- *She needs a father figure.*
- *The cultural differences are too big.*
- *The two of them are so different from each other.*
- *Their backgrounds are so different.*
- *There is such a big age gap between them.*
- *There is such a cultural difference*
- *There is such a power imbalance.*
- *They are not suited.*

These judgemental views can actually strengthen the love between two people rather than corrode it. The power of a genuine love acts as the force of connection, despite the minds of others, whether family, friends or colleagues. Love takes priority even if it fades in due course and one has to weather the snide remarks of "I told you so."

Religion and Eros

Years ago, I recall inviting a friend, a Western Theravada Abbot who had been ordained for around 15 years, to offer him and a novice a meal at my home. We were talking about life as a Buddhist monk in the West. He told me he remained a 'faithful disciple' of his teachers, Ajahn Chah of North East Thailand and Ajahn Sumedho, formerly the Abbot of Amaravati Monastery in Hertfordshire in southern England.

The following year the Abbot failed to come down for the main meal in his small monastery in Switzerland. Other monks, nuns and laypeople waited for him. He didn't appear. One of the monks knocked gently on his door. There was no reply. He opened the door. On the table, the Abbot had folded his monk's robes with a brief note on top. It said the immortal words. "I have left the discipline." The monk had fallen in love and left secretly with his beloved. One of the monks told me later that he was baffled as to how the Abbot developed such love. Under the discipline, a monk cannot speak with a woman alone. There has to be a third person present.

I regarded the event, and the manner of his departure, as a beautiful and romantic story in the best traditions of Romeo and Juliet. Others thought differently. Sadly, the Abbot who listened to his heart died within a few years from the effects of an old bullet wound in the back of his head. He had been shot while out on patrol in the jungle as a soldier in the American war against the people of Vietnam. He had left Vietnam to join the army of the ordained Buddhist monks in Thailand. He was a remarkable man. He knew the power of love.

As religion, with its often crippling morality, disappears from consciousness, romantic love makes an important contribution to shaking up our lives. It shifts us out of blind routines and, most important of all, moves consciousness into the rarefied realm of the heart, deep, subtle and vulnerable. A deep love goes well beyond the habitual perception of likes and dislikes

Religion and Erotic Love

Middle East religions have little light to shed on erotic love. Judaism has made the family sacred and disregarded yogi/monastic traditions. Orthodox Jews see making love as the means for procreation. Christianity holds family and monastic life in equal regard. The Roman Catholic Church sees sexual intimacy as only for the making of children and forbids birth control. The Church imposes celibacy on all of its priests, denying them the opportunity to explore romantic love and share with their parishioners their understanding from experience. This prohibition of marriage has contributed to immense emotional problems for some priests in their relationship to men, women or children. Islam is another family tradition often with controlling views about the place of men, women and children.

We have the general impression that religion is a sexually repressive environment that imposes codes of behaviour. Hindu yogis, Buddhist monks and nuns often struggle around sexual issues as well as single people, partners and families committed to spiritual values and practices.

Some naively believe that freedom from religion liberates people from problems around sexuality - if only that was true. Secular society is as madly obsessed with sex as religion and has very little to offer in terms of a model of sexual awakening. The biggest money-spinner on the Internet is the porn industry; advertisers employ sex, more than anything else, to sell their clients' products.

Society obsesses about sex. Women and men dress to appear sexually provocative. Millions of newspapers and magazines feature sex on its front and inside pages to attract readers. The gutter press and magazines for men and women saturates pages with sex scandals of the rich and shameless. Sex is the biggest money making industry. Religion and secular society have often become caught up in either a repressive attitude towards sex or a permissive, self-indulgent attitude. There is a middle way between these two extreme which includes the celebration of love, romantic engagement and sexual intimacy as vehicles for awakening.

In the long history of Hinduism and Buddhism, Tantra emerged as a small offshoot from the main stream of spiritual/religious practices with a clear acknowledgement of the potency of sexual energy. There are some excellent Tantric teachers who guide people in skilful ways to experience and understand their sexuality. Partners benefit from Tantric retreats and courses. People who are single can develop confidence and trust in contact with another. Such workshops require the facilitator to apply ethical values and sensitivity to the feelings and personal history of participants.

Some Westerners have grabbed onto the concept, and devalued Tantra by using it as a synonym for sexual indulgence, if not rampant permissiveness, thus once again obscuring the potential for harmony and well-being around matters of sex. Giving sexual license to wild behaviour and narcissistic sex bears no relationship to the Tantra that offers a sacred approach to love and intimacy. In other words, some Tantric 'masters' have hijacked the concept of Tantra lending itself to abuse of sex, power and money. It is important to know authentic Tantra.

Meditative disciplines that demand use of control can suffocate the power of erotic love. Teachers tell yogis to observe and let go of their passionate energy as if it was an

40

inherent problem rather than a natural energy common to humanity. It is common for meditation teachers to treat the passionate energies that arise in Dharma practitioners as hindrances, obscuration or distractions. Teachers encourage their meditation students to watch the pleasurable sensations come and go, not to cling to them, so they pass away as quickly as possible. Instead of treating sexual energies as a beneficial release in meditation, we advocate neutral sensations.

Mindfulness and equanimity gain a transcendent status at the expense of love and the erotic. It may well be unhealthy to reject the passions of the inner life and the creative imagination that accompanies it. Of course, when sexual fantasy life has something violent, depraved or corrupt about it, then that certainly deserves some deep inquiry. The yogi must engage in wise counsel with the teacher or inquire deeply within.

Buddhism often seems to be out of its depth when it comes to pointing the way to the awakening potential of the experience of romantic love. Authentic intimate love can reveal the joyful and the painful within us. We need to treat sexual intimacy with the greatest respect. In the intimacy with another of heart, mind and body, we have the potential to touch very deep feelings and trigger strong emotions, welcome and unwelcome. Fears, neediness, anger, jealousy, clinging and withdrawal can impact upon consciousness, forcing us to look at the condition of our inner life.

There are plenty of couples who certainly make it clear that their relationship is part of their practice. This is commendable. There are Dharma teachers offering skilful guidance and practices for couples: equally commendable. The application of Dharma teachings to romantic love can go very deep through sharing of experiences, inner inquiry, mindfulness and respectful communication.

41

The awakening of romantic love has the potential to point the way to liberation from the mundane. Dharma includes exploration and inquiry into intimacy. Romantic love has the potential to belong to the sphere of noble realisations as much as loving kindness and other expressions of love.

The Benefits of a Committed Relationship

The Buddha pointed to the direct and meaningful benefits of being in a committed relationship. A couple, Nakulapita and Nakulamata, both dedicated to each other, told the Buddha that they "wished to be in each other's sight for as long as life lasts." The Buddha responded that they would remain together for as long as they shared the *same trust, virtue, giving, and wisdom.* This is truly sound advice for all partners, and well worth bearing in mind, not as a demand upon the partner but to ask oneself regularly questions such as:

- *In what ways do I offer trust?*
- *What virtues do we share with each other?*
- *What do we give to each other?*
- *What is the understanding and wisdom between us?*

In the Sutta the Buddha added:

"When both are faithful and bountiful
self-restrained in Dharma living
they come together as man as wife
full of love for each other.
Many blessings come their way.
They dwell together in happiness."

The Buddha emphasised the immense importance of love, loving kindness (*metta*) and deep connection with another and others. Generally speaking, the major Buddhist

42

traditions seem to have marginalised romantic love, so that it ends up on the periphery of Dharma practice. The Tibetan tradition views Tantric practices as primarily confined to meditation, rather than exploration of intimacy with another for awakening. The other Buddhist traditions, such as Theravada and Zen, need to embrace Tantra to support the Dharma practice of lovers. Love frees up the inner life, whether it is the love of solitude or the love of intimacy with another.

Common Perceptions of Romantic Love

For romantic love to receive its due acknowledgement in Dharma practice, it has hurdles to overcome in the Buddhist tradition, (which often perceives it as filled with projections, desire and various unresolved needs). This is a cold-blooded approach to Eros. A romantic human being can express a normal, healthy emotional life rich in intimacy, poetic communications and deep engagements that is, in no way, in opposition to their Dharma practice. Some serious-minded, dry and aloof meditators perceive such people as out of touch with reality. But the heavenly realms are as much a true reality as the human realm.

Owing to self-interest, there is the perception that romantic love easily leads to unconscious behaviour. Certainly romantic love is vulnerable to disappointment and hurt through projections, expectations and incapacity to deal with rejection. Hindu-Buddhist Tantric texts, poetry and plays, fiction and non-fiction, give support for the exploration, inspiration and fusion of romantic love, sexuality, energy and the arts. In the account of his night of awakening, the Buddha reported that visions of beautiful and alluring women arose in his meditations. He struggled to overcome the temptations to lose himself in sensual pleasures, especially sexual fantasies. It is written the gods were delighted in the Buddha's determination to stay true to his commitment to liberate himself from the seductive power of *Mara*. The Buddha's story stands in sharp contrast to the story of Siva in whom the gods were equally pleased.

Siva listened to his heart and trusted in it. At Mount Kailash on the Tibetan/Nepalese border, Siva engaged in austere meditation practices as a dedicated yogi until the beautiful Parvati appeared. She danced in front of Siva and then offered him a necklace of flowers. Siva came out of his deep meditation, opened his eyes and immediately fell in love with her, the most beautiful woman of the Himalayas. He got out of his full lotus position, stood up and joined Parvati in her dance. The gods were in bliss. He engaged in the ecstatic union of man and woman – the dancer and the dance were one. Siva retained all his powers as a yogi while Parvati became his shakti, the creative energy of the cosmos. Siva and Parvati were inseparable. There was no division between the yogi and the lover. This is another perspective revealing neither being lost in another nor a detachment from the other. Siva's story reminds us of our capacity for mutual awakening between two people who love each other.

Romantic Love and the Dating Agency

Owing to busy lives, stress and lack of self-confidence, the search for an encounter with romantic love moves more and more from the 'real' world to the Internet. Clients of dating agencies hope they will find that special person through the agency. The online agencies seem to have become the Western form of the arranged marriage. If the individual unconsciously sees the agency as a kind of parenting process, he or she will transfer many of the risks and responsibilities for any consequences of a date, positive or negative, to the dating agency.

The dating agency will invite the person who is looking for a relationship, for marriage, to complete a lengthy questionnaire involving countless details of their client's personal life with a view to matching them up with someone for the long term. There is a possibility that the client seeks an agency as a form of risk aversion, perhaps forgetting that information about self and other cannot safeguard the inner life from hurt, disappointment and judgemental views. An estimated one in four clients have little interest in developing a long term relationship but simply enjoy dating and the possibility of a sexual encounter. For more and more people, online dating has become a form of recreational activity.

Love invites an ongoing risk. The deeper we dive into love then the deeper the risk we take. Love requires the ongoing support of fearless communication, clarity of mind and equanimity around outcome of giving love to another.

The agency matches up the necessary details, and arranges for the couple to meet. Perhaps the meeting will spark mutual passions? Perhaps the meeting will spark passion for one and not the other or for neither of two people. The agency aims to minimise the possibility of a problematic encounter by ensuring a commonality of shared interests, but love for another (or for a cause) cannot offer such safety and security.

Real love entails an adventure, a sense of walking to the edge of the known and the unknown without traces of ongoing security. Such love confirms the spiritual sensitivities of the human being. The intensity of the initial romantic encounter can develop the willingness to sustain love against the odds. We might want to find another who thinks, looks and lives similar to ourselves. This approach could recourse to safety rather than an adventure into the exploration of romantic involvement. Not surprisingly, online dating can bring couples together, time after time, in the belief that a match will occur. The failure rate is high since the abstraction of common details, or what the one seeks, may have little relevance to a real encounter when love fuses with romantic passion for the long term.

While recognising the thoughtful concerns of the agencies and the clients to ensure safety, we might ask whether the safety element actually inhibits the power of love, its urgency and its insecurity. Are the dating agencies agents of love or only offering the satisfaction of romantic friendships: polite, convenient and passive?

Abiding with depth, a genuine love requires a regular revitalisation from for renewal, passion, and further extension of love. A habitual togetherness eats away at real love until all that remains is a polite friendship, a numbness of the heart's passion, warfare behind closed doors or open warfare. The principle of revitalisation of love applies equally to lovers, friends, family and the collective (the group, the faith, the organisation and the political party).

Our encounter with love guards against the predominance of self-interest: of placing oneself before all else. Self-interest defies love, inhibiting its expression owing to excessive attention to personal desires, if not demands. We need not elevate love into a great metaphysical concept (e.g. God is Love) but we explore the experience and language of love, while taking into equal consideration truth, the bare reality and the situational experience.

In relationship, love requires skilful reflection on the past to see where we stayed true to love, and where we departed from love into harmful and unhealthy patterns of behaviour. It is foolish to engage in the glorification of love since love then becomes isolated from the field of causation.

46

We notice that we can experience love in a way that we could never imagine. It manifests in the most unexpected ways out of the dynamics of daily life. The capacity to stay true to love requires much in the way of understanding ourselves, others and situations and we equally acknowledge that we cannot make sense of love, of what we feel. Once the person takes the other or the situation for granted, then love will drift into a passive acceptance and the questionable security of a habit. Love needs the willingness to be present, vital and feel connected with another in a conscious and obvious way.

Taking Risks

Love means the act of taking risks. For some, the risk involves contacting a dating agency and relaying information about oneself in order to secure a date. For others, it is the willingness to initiate a conversation with another with whom there is, at least, a minimum of romantic curiosity. It would be hard to imagine a love without boldness. No matter how deep, love does not offer any assurance that it will be reciprocated. It might seem brutally unfair that love sometimes goes in one direction and not be returned. The reliance upon a reciprocated love does not constitute a deep love, but the all-too-human needs of the self for personal affirmation. In such situations, the self serves as the agent to undermine the very foundations of love.

Emerging from an experience or situation, the power of love has this incredible to breathe new life into that which was previously unseen. Love has the fragrance and the immediacy of freshly cut grass. We undermine love when we rely upon the past for its sustenance.

A woman in Germany had been dating a man for some months. They met through a dating agency. She could not make up her mind whether he was the right man for her or could she find a better man through the agency. One Sunday afternoon they hired a canoe on a small lake. As he rowed the canoe, she looked to him and the thought arose in her mind: "Why on earth am I looking for another man? He is a beautiful human being."

In that moment a real and enduring love emerged from the situation enabling her to experience the freedom within to commit to deepening their relationship. That moment shaped the rest of her life. They married within weeks. Such moments carry a mystery, an inexplicable insight or intuition. We can say there is something spiritual in the transformative moment of such a spark of awakening.

The core mystery of romantic love, of the actualisation of Eros, shows itself in the unpredictable and formidable appearance of the spark. This spark lights the fire between two people or one person to the other. Contingency factors can co-operate together, with or without the assistance of the dating agency, but no supplementary conditions whatsoever can trigger the spark that leads to the fire of passionate romance. The spark initiates the visceral sensations, the first-hand experience of intimacy, and a willingness to go further and deeper than before. Nobody can organise this critical feature of causation that illuminates consciousness so that the immediate world of the other appears in new light.

Others may not recall a spark, either on their first date, nor weeks nor months later, but recognise a gradually deepening of their love for the other. The deepening of love also conveys the sense of the spiritual.

Pleasure and Love

Pleasure easily gets confused with love. The distinction between the two needs to be made clear. The field of pleasure

48

is the desirable outcome of an intention that the self has pursued. A desirable outcome, gives pleasure, long or short lasting. Pleasure remains bounds to feelings, to sensations, whereas love remains free from any restriction to such feelings. Love does not fall into the 'endgame' category but, with the support of ethics, but is willing to venture into a brave new world. The capacity to stay totally committed to acts of love includes the random events, or the intended events, spontaneous situations or planned in advance, the personal or political.

We may experience a great deal of pleasure and satisfaction in a sexual encounter but sexual engagement does not generally lead to love, since love expresses the capacity to give rather than get. The pursuit of another's love fails to confirm our love but confirms our desire for another for our satisfaction. We know love when we see through questionable thought processes and reflect on our desires, and show equal concern for the other. Such love manifests in words, actions and touch. The sexual encounter is a confirmation of love not an action to find love. Seduction obscures the beauty of love since the desire to have power over the other rests in priority being given to the needs of the self.

Owing to Ancient Greek influence, we make a distinction between romantic love (*Eros*) and fraternal love (*filia*). Religions have tended to lean strongly towards *filia* and regarded *Eros* as problematic. The meeting of *Eros* and the fraternal frequently overlap in the intimacies of passion and friendship – with or without sensual touch. Such an encounter of *Eros* and *filia* certainly requires vigilance from two people who feel both for each other but know it is unwise to develop the sensual aspects further. These encounters of intimacy confirm love as much more than temporary pleasurable feelings since the real encounter becomes an event that can actively alter the priorities of our lives.

49

Two people often sense that they share the potential to do much together. Partners also have to remember that they have to make personal sacrifices for each other. At times, they will need to negotiate together on mattes that affect both of them. The single person does not have to engage in a dialogue with another about a decision making process: moving home, buying new furniture or visiting relatives. Our time with the other means less time for something else.

Love expresses the gift of presence and the capacity for letting go, for renunciation of personal needs. The confirmation of love moves through the two fields of experience – to give and to let go. Love has the capacity for endurance in these two fields. Two people, or a group of people with a shared vision, empower each other through a meditation on love and an inquiry into its purpose for a supreme way of life.

The Brief Encounter

One woman told me that she and an American Dharma teacher experienced strong attraction towards each other during a retreat. She simply did not know whether she had become caught up in what we sometimes call a 'Vipassana Romance' – charged full of projections, passion and stimulating sensations - or whether her experience of the teacher had some depth of mutual interest, an acknowledgment of the beginnings of romantic love. She sensed from the regularity of their eye contact, the longer interviews and the glimpse of recognition between them in the hall that some chemistry was arising between them. After the retreat, they kept in contact and later met to spend a day together that resulted in making love in her flat. It didn't go any further than that. She told me that she knew she could get the teacher into an enormous amount of trouble with the

Buddhist retreat centre who invited him to teach, if she made a formal complaint about him. She knew it would have led to the board of the centre banning the teacher from teaching there and other Buddhist centres would probably have done the same.

She said: "Our day of lovemaking turned out to be a huge blessing for me. I felt empowered and totally loved as a woman. Afterwards I was able to take full responsibility for my part in our day of passion. I did not get caught up in moralizing about him abusing his role or taking advantage of my vulnerability on retreat. Since then I have regarded myself as a much more mature woman. I now have very occasional contact with the teacher. I have been on retreat with him since. We have become friends."

The woman showed a mature response in taking her share of responsibility. The same situation could have ended up as a nightmare for all involved including herself, the teacher and the centre. On reflection, she might have felt vulnerable and exploited. She might have felt that there was a great power imbalance on the retreat which he used for his advantage. She took a positive view.

Extract from a poem:

A Meeting in Love

I want you to walk about in my heart,
to stroll around within me,
to visit any forgotten corners of my inner life,

A partner may move on – not out of anger or blame, nor due to betrayal, nor due to disillusionment, but simply as she or he stays true to the inner voice for the next step in awakening.

There are many considerations for a couple totally committed together to the relationship as a path to Awakening. Aspects of deep communication between a Dharma teacher and students, or deep spiritual friends, equally apply in marriage or partnership, including:

- *Communicating what is true and useful*
- *Discussion of the Dharma and giving support to the partner's exploration*
- *Engaging in acts of generosity and kindness*
- *Expressing love through words and touch daily*
- *Living a lifestyle of easy maintenance*
- *Not raising the voice, not speaking impatiently*
- *Really listening to each other*
- *Recognising time to be alone and time to be with each other*
- *Sharing experiences together to contribute to mutual awakening*

The Buddhist tradition has not placed emphasis on marriage as either religious or sacred. Theravada monks are not permitted to act in the role of a priest who marries couples and marriage services do not take place in monasteries. Marriage is purely a secular event where a man and woman, or same sex couples, announce publicly their commitment to each other. There is nothing innately religious or spiritual about this public agreement between two people. It is a social contract between the two parties concerned. Equally, separation and divorce bears no religious significance either. If the marriage fails to work, then the two people take the necessary steps towards mutual friendship, and practice to continue to show loving kindness towards each other and any children. Two unmarried people who share the same bed, whether of both sexes or the same sex, cannot 'live in sin' in the Buddhist tradition.

Dharma teachings do not swallow the commonly held religious standpoint that God acts as a witness to marriage vows. It may not be wise to take a vow such as 'until death do us part'. Love and understanding uphold a contented marriage, not a belief in God or marriage as a religious institution. Marriage as a legal contract, neither contributes to wisdom nor impedes. It neither is essential for awakening nor blocks it; neither enhances liberation nor denies it. There is far too much projection into marriage – either for it or against it.

Greek Mythology also endorses romantic love as a path of awakening. Ancient Greeks reminded us that Eros bereft of Psyche (Love without the Mind) falls into unhappiness. The story of Eros and Psyche reports the significance of the struggle that takes place between the two of them. Jealous of the mortal beauty of Psyche, Aphrodite tells her son, Eros, to cause Psyche to fall in love with the ugliest being on earth. Obeying his mother, Eros took two vials of potion for Psyche to swallow so that men would avoid her. Unmindfully, he managed to prick Psyche with his arrow and this made her fall in love with him instantly. Eros was overwhelmed with her beauty and so pricked himself. It was love at first sight for both of them.

Then Eros leaves Psyche and she wanders around the world looking for him for love. Eros tells Psyche she must descend into the Underworld (the Unconscious) and make contact with the Gods. The Gods tell Psyche to go the top of a mountain and there she will find Eros. Love and Mind are reconciled. There is a transcendent power when these two forces meet each other. Psyche and Eros meet today to form a relationship. One partner primarily acts from her or his heart. The other partner primarily acts from her or his mind. For some couples, it is a partnership made in heaven. For other couples........!

Buddhist Institutions

Some sincere Buddhists treat sexual intercourse as gross. As a result, there is often a negative standpoint towards those who explore a completely different ethic in matters of sexuality. Views about celibacy are the weakest link in the Buddhist tradition leading to the separation of one identity (the practising celibate), from another identity (the person in a sexual relationship). Today, this is a different era. The celibate and the lover share equal opportunities for awakening. This is a clear departure from the view in the East. The act of making love is true Dharma in accordance with the intimacy of organic life, not an activity to transcend.

In the Buddhist tradition the problematic concept is desire (the word used to translate the Pali concept *tanha* – meaning desire, craving, thirsting after). On face value, it would seem impossible to make love without desire. *Tanha* carries within it the message of unsatisfactoriness, suffering and a problematic movement of the inner life. Certainly selfish desire can enter into sexual activity, such as:

- *the pursuit of sexual satisfaction,*
- *forcing another to submit,*
- *a lack of respect for another,*
- *the sexual exploitation of vulnerability of another,*
- *taking risks around sexually transmitted diseases.*

In this context, the word *tanha* addresses the range of unsatisfactory movement in thought, word and action, especially suffering associated with sex. We can make love without *tanha,* that is without desire. We then make love with love and wise intention. We make love with passion, kindness and creativity. We make love with the heart, with poetic language and with sensitive touch. There is the potential for an explosion of mutually appreciative joy, the fullness of intimate action and deep insights. In the act of making love, there is the power of trust, mindfulness, concentration, energy and wisdom – what the Buddha referred to as the Five Powers. Desire is not necessary to make love. Love makes love.

Desire is a different force altogether from the movement of love. Sexual desire creates problems for the one with the desire and for the one who is the object of desire. There is a world of difference between making love and having sex. There is a different movement between making love without desire between two people and having sex through desire. The difference is critical: it is the difference between the wisdom of love and *tanha* revealed as a selfish pursuit of personal satisfaction or gratification. Wisdom distinguishes between the two as both can fuse while making love.

It is vital to listen equally to the responses of the partner prior to such intimacy, throughout the entire act and subsequently, as much as listening to ourselves. It is a path of mutual awakening.

EXTRACT FROM A POEM – THE MEETING POINT

the ocean held them in its sway
as they sat on the edge of eternity,
turning their eye in the direction of the rolling wave
as total presence descended upon them,
like the white spray of energised waves

From Poems from the Edge of Time.

It is an essential practice of a meditator to know the difference in the intensity of pleasant sensations between the formations of personal desire (with its need for self-gratification, gross or subtle), and the expression of love. Desire distorts love. There are differences in the actual sensations in the body and feelings between desire and love. I" "me" and "my" infect the act of making love. Desire and love are a different experience.

Those who have dissolved the poisonous drive of desire know love and liberation and are no longer a slave to desire. Real love has a free movement, without the desire to take advantage of another or a situation. Respect and sensitivity support this love. The heart knows intimacy and emancipation belong to each other.

Chapter 3

The Power of Friendship (*Metta*)

Look at those who struggle after their petty ambitions like fish in a stream fast drying up. Seeing this, let one abide unselfish. Sn 776.

In a much loved passage, the Buddha uttered a clear statement of the significance of a noble and profound friendship in a conversation with his attendant, Ananda, who referred to such a friendship as "half the reason for the spiritual life." The Buddha replied: 'Don't say that, Ananda. Don't say that. Noble friendship is the whole of the spiritual life. When one has such friends, one can develop the path. (SN.45.2)."

The Buddha employed the word *metta* (Sanskrit – *matri*) which means friendship, love and loving kindness. To abide in deep *metta* is to abide in the Divine (*Brahma Vihara*), he said.

The Buddha also said on another occasion: 'With regard to external factors, I do see any other single factor like noble friendship as doing so much for one who has not attained the heart's goal. One who is a friend with noble people abandons what is unskilful and develops what is skilful. (Iti 1.17)

The Buddha said that a profound friendship contributes to an ethical way of life, generosity and discernment of what matters. Through a noble friendship one can discover release from being trapped in grasping birth, ageing, pain and death. He added: "This is why a deep friendship is the whole of the spiritual life." (AN 8.54).

Metta also expresses as love, loving kindness, expressions of respect and acts revealing a deep empathy for others. For the Buddha, our steadfast friendship for others confirms our humanity and our divine nature. In spiritual language, a divine friendship (*metta brahma vihara*) signifies the meeting of the gods with the human world. As earthly creatures, we confirm the divine through the opening up of our heart.

A deep friendship is a powerful force that sweeps away negativity, envy and indifference. It sometimes emerges out of deep realisations, insights into the nature of things and the authentic freedom of the heart. This friendship reveals itself equally in personal relationships, lifestyle and social/political concerns, as well as acts of selfless kindness towards people, animals and the environment.

Authors, poets, playwrights, film makers and song writers remind humanity, with an unflagging consistency, of the significance of *metta* and the vulnerabilities that accompany matters of the heart, such as rejection, separation or death. Great religious texts carry the message of love and deep friendship of those who share a similar vision. Such friendship between those who share a profound vision can matter even at the cost of their own lives. Friendship can take priority over everything else.

It is our task to make friendship with ethics, wise discernment and skilful action a guiding force, a reference point for what we say and what we do so that friendliness bears an influence on thoughts, words and deeds. The Buddha calls upon people to express this friendship without limits, so that it pervades conscious life as a divine and enduring element. The experience of this divine friendship arises through creativity, meditation, nature and contact with sentient and insentient life. We have the capacity to know and experience it on a daily basis, not as an infrequent occurrence. At its best, religion, psychology, education and the arts can play an important role through reminding us of the transformative power of loving kindness.

The current explanations and literature on divine friendship (*metta*) in the Buddhist tradition often falls far short of the expansive significance of *metta*. This is partly due the narrow translation of the word '*metta*' as 'loving kindness' rather than communicating the full range of the experience of *metta* to include love, friendship and a deep empathy with life. The full translation of *metta* expresses itself as limitless friendship, unconditional love and boundless expressions of loving kindness. Through the power of such *metta*, we abide in the divine *(brahma vihara)*. Metta communicates different expressions of friendship and love according to the situation.

There is also romantic love with a partner, passionate and intimate. There is protective love of parents to children, the devotional love of follower to guru. There is the love expressed through true friendship between two or more people. There is love in generosity *(dana)* and acts of sharing. There is love of Dharma practice as an expression of love for oneself. There is love of animals and nature. There is love of liberation and love of vision.

Metta shows itself as acts of service. The Buddha said *metta* travels in all directions Metta extends itself to all life including humans, creatures in the air, in the water, on the ground and forms living under the ground. A deep friendship for sentient beings springs from selfless considerations. It is an unconditional friendship not a love dependent on the condition of our personality or on the behaviour of others.

Metta and the Buddhist Tradition

There is a common belief in the Theravada tradition of Buddhism that *metta* is primarily a meditation practice. Buddhist commentaries claim *metta* meditation practice leads to *Samadhi* (meditative concentration) because the mind relaxes through loving kindness meditation: the heart feels good and it is easier to concentrate on a meditation object. While the development of kindness, inwardly and outwardly, in meditation, functions as a supportive condition for meditative concentration (*samadhi*), such meditation practice hardly qualifies as a divine abiding. This view neglects the profound significance of *metta* where human consciousness becomes divine through a life totally dedicated to an unshakeable friendship, even when facing rejection, betrayal or abandonment.

We can confuse *metta* meditations with warm, pervasive oceanic feelings when our meditations make no difference to daily relationships. The power of love includes feeling good about others and ourselves but does not depend on such feelings for its expression. The divine is more profound than that. *Metta* requires a selfless dedication, a steadfast commitment to stay true to love, to friendship, regardless of how much rejection we have to endure.

Furthermore, there is no guarantee that Buddhist *metta* meditation practices lead to the *Brahma Viharas* (Divine Abiding, the Kingdom of God, Home of the Gods) unless the force and the power of friendship moves consciousness out of the attachment to pleasurable sensations and the desire to be liked and wanted. Metta directs the heart towards the happiness and clarity of others, even at personal cost or personal risk. Traditional loving kindness meditations only point the way to divine love in the same way a view of the Himalayas is not the same as standing on a Himalayan peak!

In a traditional *metta* meditation, the meditator will direct loving kindness towards the three kinds of people in their world: the friendly people, the unfriendly people and strangers. The real challenge is maintaining direct contact regularly with these three kinds of people in the world as expression of loving kindness. Meditation practices to develop a depth of friendship serves as a beginners' step towards being at home with the divine. *Metta* meditation serves as a worthwhile preparatory practice for going deeper into the heart of the reality of situations.

There is nowhere in his discourses that the Buddha offered a method and technique to develop *metta*. The modern concept of *metta* has become a practice to generate loving feelings to oneself and then to the three categories of people. These people sometimes receive far less time as recipients of *metta* compared to the amount of loving kindness the meditator gives to herself or himself. If a practice of *metta* becomes primarily for oneself it gets uncomfortably close to the point of a narcissistic self-absorption, and yet there is a place for this given the self-hatred that plagues the inner life of so many people.

The same principle applies to the beneficial practice of compassion for oneself in the Buddhist tradition, employed by those who constantly give themselves a hard time. The Buddha regarded divine compassion as the direct action to relieve or resolve suffering near or far, inwardly and outwardly.

Abiding in the Divine (Brahma Vihara)

Devout Hindus believed that unity with the Supreme showed the highest attainment – a view also shared with devout believers of monotheistic religions in India and elsewhere. The Buddha disputed this view of the self's absorption into God as the ultimate aim of humanity. Instead he made clear the power of *metta*, of a deep and unshakeable friendship, as something divine to apply in all directions. It means consciousness dwells full of love without even making a claim to a Supreme.

Despite his shift away from the orthodoxy of religious beliefs, the Buddha retained the conventional religious language of abiding in the divine as a skilful means to support release of the heart from pain to love. This may not sit easily with strictly non-theistic Buddhists so some Buddhist translators have translated the word *"Brahma"* as 'Sublime', but this misses the point of the Buddha's wise application of religious language to those who appreciate such concepts. Rather than reject the notion of the Divine or God, he reinterpreted such concepts and applied them to the depths of kindness and compassion, appreciative joy and a profound equanimity in the face of challenging circumstances.

Our experiences can empower friendship to act as a moving and transformative force. The divinity of unwavering friendliness confirms an extraordinarily expansive heart amidst the most challenging of circumstances, between birth and death. In the Parable of the Saw (MN 21) the Buddha exhorted the monk Phagguna to know divine friendship.

"If anyone were to reproach you right to your face... give you a blow with the hand, or hit you with a clod of earth, or with a stick, or with a sword, even then you should abandon (reactive) urges. Train yourself: 'Neither shall my mind be affected by this, nor shall I give vent to evil words; but I shall remain with a mind of friendship, and I shall not give in to hatred.'

The Buddha told the Sangha that *"even if bandits were to sever you limb by limb with a double-handled saw, you should not give way to hatred but must develop boundless friendship towards the bandits, as well as the entire world."*

The Buddha encouraged the discovery of the power p of friendship and the depths of kindness, even if facing a painful death from persecution. Few people will ever face such challenges. Yet, there are people in the spotlight who have to deal with character assassination, ridicule and condemnation even though they have not caused harm to anyone. Some show remarkable fortitude in the abuse hurled at them from television, radio, newspapers and social media. This requires a friendly attitude and a capacity to abide in a divine equanimity (*upekkha brahma vihara*). Others fine themselves under arrest, facing long term imprisonment, solitary confinement and ill treatment for their non-violent beliefs or through innocence. Such men and women also need friendliness and equanimity, otherwise they will burn up inside with resentment. If this happens, the media or the authorities have got a grip on the heart of that person. One Palestinian, a non-violent activist, told me after his release after 10 years in an Israeli political prison: "The State can take everything away from you. But they can't take away your inner freedom if you don't react to their determination to humiliate you."

Such divine love earns deep respect from many. It is an extra-ordinary attainment for a human being to know such a divinity of experience through deep friendship, compassion, appreciative joy and equanimity. Realising our divinity serves as a truly transformative force on perceptions, values and daily priorities.

God and the Divine

The image of the God of the monotheistic Middle Eastern religions is absolute, all-powerful and patriarchal. In ancient India, *Brahma* is GOD amongst the Gods. It is important to distinguish the difference. The God of the Middle East is a Creator God who dispenses rewards and punishment for beliefs and behaviour. In Hinduism, Brahma is also the Creator God, a personification of any creative process going back in time from sub-atomic particle, the Big Bang and evolutionary life. In India, Brahma co-exists with Vishnu, the God who sustains, and Siva, the God of the end, destruction and death, (from an extinguished candle flame to the loss of life). The Buddha took the personification of these forces out of his teachings and referred instead to arising, staying and passing. At the time of the Buddha, people worshipped Brahma with the Brahmins as the representatives of God on Earth.

The Buddha showed little regard for this belief in an all-powerful Brahma and the priestly class of the Brahmins and instead concentrated on the divinity of profound expressions of love, compassion, appreciative joy and equanimity.

Love has the extraordinary capacity to go far beyond all limits and boundaries that the individual tries to set. The Buddha said: *"With a mind full of love (metta), one pervades the whole world with friendship/love/kindness."(See Buddhist Dictionary, Nyanatiloka).*

'Friendship is conducive to unity' (MLD 104).

The Buddha made frequent reference to *'liberation of the heart and mind through love (metta ceto-vimutti) and metta-sahagatena cetasa - with a heart and mind full of love (D.1.250).'*

Throughout the discourses *(suttas)*, we find regular references to love as a vehicle for transformation. Here are a few examples. Sometimes, it is worthwhile reading slowly to see if the words offer inspiration or insight. We easily gloss over words that might reveal a deeper truth.

"The liberation of heart and mind by metta shines forth, bright and brilliant."

"By this liberation through love, one leaves nothing untouched, nothing unaffected in the sensuous sphere. This is the way to union with Brahma."

"The brightness of being that emerges through liberation by love shines 16 times more strongly than the sun, the moon and the morning." (It. 27. 19-21)

A young Brahmin, Subha, asked Gautama *"the way to be with God."* The Buddha gave him a very different interpretation of dwelling with *Brahma* than the Brahminical belief in the union of the soul with God *(Atman and Brahman)*.

The Buddha replied: *"A man who has come from the village of Nalakara would be able to point the way to the village for others. Would that man be slow to answer?*

Subha agreed that the man could easily and quickly point the way. The Buddha said he knew the way to the Divine –*"through liberation of heart/mind through love, compassion, appreciative joy and equanimity."* (MLD.99)

In the exchange with Subha, a young Brahmin, the Buddha did not attempt to refute *Brahma*, known in India as the creator God. He could have tried to explain to Subha that there was no Creator God. He could have told him Brahma was a religious myth. He acknowledged the sincerity of the question and supported the young man's earnest quest to find *Brahma* and unite with *Brahma*. The Buddha recognised the importance of the religious quest, even though he offered a different priority. He praised Brahmins for their tradition and encouraged people to offer gifts (*dana*) to other traditions, gurus and the priestly class. The Buddha displayed exceptional kindness towards the diversity of spiritual practices in India.

The Buddha emphasised a total liberation: not bound to a religious experience, or a construct of unity of the self with God or the unity of the self with the rest of life. Freedom from holding onto an experience and freedom from making an identity out of an experience (such as "I have found God" or "I am One with Everything") were important aspects of the Buddha's Dharma.

In a celebrated text in the first discourse of the *Longer Discourses of the Buddha*, the Buddha also described the widespread belief in both God (*Brahma*) and the belief in self who finds God as two unconducive views (*miccha ditthi*) to total awakening to Truth and reality. Such claims easily feed the ego. There are gurus, prophets and preachers who claim to be one with God or messengers of God and expect their disciples to obey them because of their personal claims around God. The Buddha dispensed with such God language and religions that emerged out such a language.

Referring to the Divine, the Buddha said God speaks of himself in the following way:

"I am God (Brahma), the Great God, the Conqueror, the Unconquered, the All-Seeing, the All-Powerful, the Lord, the Maker and Creator, Ruler, Appointer and Order, Father of All That Have Been and Shall Be. I created these beings.

How so? Because I first had this thought: Oh, if only some other beings would come here.´ That was my wish, and then these other beings came into this existence!"

"That God, He made us, and He is permanent, stable, eternal not subject to change. We who were created by Brahma, we are impermanent, unstable, short-lived, fated to fall away, and we have come to this world."

The Buddha did not believe in the prevailing monotheistic view that a permanent God chose to create impermanent human beings while He remained the only permanence. Yet, the Buddha still supported the quest to experience Brahma since seekers might abide (*viharati*) in a

66

divine love, compassion, appreciative joy and equanimity. He did not regard belief in God as a Person as revealing an ultimate and liberating wisdom.

Compassion, Appreciative Joy and Equanimity

A divine abiding can strip away notions of a personal God who desires the presence of loving souls, so there is access to love in ordinary situations of daily life. This depth sets no limit, and remains free from any kind of measurement or limitation. Such realisations confirm the liberating depths accessible to a human being.

Along with the divine abiding of deep friendship, compassion and appreciative joy, there is equanimity which means a deep inner peace when confronted with a difficult situation or a sudden impulse. I recall a monk in our monastery, Wat Chai Na in Nakornsridhammaraj, southern Thailand, sitting under a tree meditating. Some dogs in the monastery were chasing a poisonous snake across the grounds. The monk kept his peace as the fearful snake weaved its way towards the monk, finally taking refuge up his sarong. Monks wear nothing under their sarong. The dogs kept running around the monk in circles and barking with the snake curled up inside the crossed legs of the monk. The monk kept his equanimity.

An hour or two later, the snake quietly departed from under the robe and the monk was unharmed. Several decades ago, another Buddhist monk in northern Thailand waded into a river to bathe, not realising that crocodiles lived in the river. One crocodile glided towards him. The monk quietly chanted as the jaws of the crocodile pressed on his stomach. The Buddha gave equal emphasis to the power of equanimity as love, compassion and appreciative joy. Buddhist monks and nuns have always shared the view that no harm can come from animals, reptiles or insects if one abides in the divinity of love and equanimity with the capacity to stay calm and clear rather than frozen in fear and running away.

We, as an individual, or group or species, show our best through acts of friendship, of love, of kindness and wisdom. If belief in God gives support to the expansive depths of the caring heart, then the belief is welcome. If believe in atheism/secularism gives support to an intolerant heart, then then the heart needs reflection, meditation and expansion.

Chapter 4

Do You Have Anything Worth Giving To Others?

Trust is the best wealth. Dharma *practice brings the most happiness. Truth is the sweetest of tastes. Living with wisdom is the noblest kind of life.* Sn.182

A gift makes life a beautiful experience. A gift fills the heart with appreciative joy. A gift expresses the act of love through a form, material or immaterial. A gift benefits the giver and the receiver. A gift confirms the human capacity for selfless action. *Dana* is a Pali word meaning gift, acts of generosity or a donation. The Buddha said "The gift *(dana) of* Dharma is the best of gifts."

The insights that emerge from Dharma teachings and practices express in acts of generosity *(dana).*

There are those who truly stretch themselves in their willingness to give. They offer their services; they give of their time and make immense sacrifices. They give through their presence, through their acts, and they dig deep into their pockets to support what matters to them. Some have little and in remarkable ways will give all that they have. The willingness to devote themselves in terms of service to others shows the power of trust in themselves and the benefit for others. Those who give of themselves know there is little point of any anticipation that these acts of selflessness will provide a reward for themselves in the present or the future. They see and recognise a need and take steps to reduce or end that need.

At times, approaches to the individual or group serve as the vital catalyst for the acts of generosity. The explanation of the need triggers the loving and generous response, while others see the need and offer to give before anyone raises the matter. The time for giving needs to run close to the present moment. If we postpone the act of giving, other tasks occupy our mind so the application of *dana* takes second place, a lesser priority.

The practice of giving, and it is a practice, makes us fit and able for the task, if not the responsibility, to offer services to others, to the Earth. It is far too easy to blame others who take rather than give, or show an indifference to the capacity to donate services, immaterial and material, to others. It is the wise heart that knows the significance of giving, born out of emotional intelligence and humility, rather than pride. The wise have realised the importance of the gift. When a human being undergoes an inner transformation, he or she becomes an instrument of a divine abiding where the act of giving seeks no gratification for itself.

The wealthy can offer large sums of money for major projects. Yes, these sums usually belong to a disposable income, due to excess of profits or accumulated wealth, gradually or suddenly. These acts of generosity enable major projects to take place and there is much to be grateful for. These substantial donations from the wealthy indicate they are taking important steps towards the transformation of their lives through giving. It is a step in a noble direction.

The wealthy should take note, however, of the words of the Buddha.

"Riches ruin the foolish but not those in quest of the beyond.
By desiring riches, the witless person ruins himself as well as others." (Dh.355)

Dharma teachings do not make the simple assertion that it is good to give but also inquire into the nature of the act of giving and the various intentions that support the gift. There is the relationship formed between the giver and the receiver and the benefits of such exchange. Giving and receiving are opportunities equally for self-inquiry.

Acts of generosity can spring from healthy, unhealthy or mixed motives. The Buddha inquired into the common motives behind the act of giving, of *dana*. He referred to eight ways where the giver needs to inquire into the underlying influences for the giving.

1. *to insult*
2. *out of fear*
3. *someone has given me a gift, so I must give one in return*
4. *to give in order to get something back*
5. *to give because its considered good*
6. *it is not proper to refuse to give*
7. *to get a good reputation*
8. *to feel good about oneself (A IV 236)*

Many Dharma teachers offer the Dharma as an expression of *dana* and the listeners give, as *dana*, various forms of practical support for the teachings. *Dana* belongs to the Buddha's strategy to encourage letting go, thus ensuring that giving and service have a pre-eminent place in the Dharma (It.26:18-19). The Buddha said that if people knew the benefit of giving and sharing, they would not eat without having given, even if it were their last morsel. Happiness, peace of mind and the development of friendship come from acts of *dana*.

A beautiful statement on *dana* found in the Pali Commentaries of the Theravada Tradition, reads:

"The Great Person does not give unwillingly
Nor by afflicting others
Nor out of fear

Nor moral shame
Or the scolding of those in need of gifts.
With the excellent, he does not give what is mean.
He does not give extolling himself and disparaging others,
He does not give out of desire for the fruit,
Nor with loathing for those who ask
Nor with lack of consideration
Rather, he gives with his own hand at the proper time,
He gives with discrimination filled with joy
Having given, he does not become remorseful afterwards.
He does not become obsequious with recipients
But behaves amiably towards them.
Bountiful and liberal, he gives."

From the Cariyapitika Atthakatha. Translated by
Bhikkhu Bodhi.

The Buddha spoke of *saddaya danam deti* – to give with confidence and trust. He made it abundantly clear that it is worthwhile to give to the Sangha of noble men and women through acts of support and hospitality. The giver of *dana* makes merit – meaning the giver experiences benefits as well as the receiver. "*A deed of merit brings one happiness*", said the Buddha. The giver develops ethics, values and happiness through acts of generosity. There are noble men and women who give their lives in extreme situations for the welfare of others. This is the greatest of all gifts, the greatest *dana* of all. Those who sacrifice their lives for others do so in the confidence and trust that it brings direct benefit for another or others.

The Sangha of teachers and yogis endeavor to ensure acts of giving sustain the teachings. Compared to the sacrifice of one's life as a *dana*, other forms of *dana* may seem less significant. It is not wise to compare one *dana* with another since it easily leads to praise and blame, approval and disapproval, satisfaction and dissatisfaction. Risks take place every time acts of giving arise whether giving money, time, services or presence. For example, sometimes the Sangha offers retreats totally in return for *dana* while organisers and teachers would be accountable for any financial shortfall. Others may give an enormous amount of time and energy to a project that eventually falls apart. There are some of the risks in giving. There is the sincere wish for something to come out of the action, but there are no guarantees. Despite such vulnerability, the act of the gift shows the selflessness of the individual or group, and trust in the value of the expression of love and service. The Buddha took into consideration the circumstances of the individual when he emphasized the practice of *dana* in his teachings.

The Buddha endorsed a basic lifestyle for the Sangha and Dharma*salas* (Dharma centres) to keep such environments simple and sustainable. He advocated *dana* to serve as an antidote to selfish desire which contains the intention to take from the word more than we need. In the 45 years that the Buddha walked the length and breadth of the Sakya kingdom and neighbouring countries, his students were often referred to as '*savakas*' – meaning 'the practitioners who listen' (to the Dharma). *Upasaka* is the Pali word for *householders who follow the* Dharma. ('*upa*' – 'up close' '*as*' – 'to sit') *Upasakas* are men and women who *sit up close and listen* to the Dharma teachings that the teacher offers without charge. Householders and wandering nomads sat close and gave their hearts and minds to listen, practice and share experiences. This process supported letting go of problematic mind sets, especially clinging, to release greater acts of giving. Since *dana* relates directly to ethics, practice and values, it supports the taking of risks through unmeasured giving. The Buddha said:

"Some provide from the little they have
Others who are affluent don't like to give
An offering given from what little one has
Is worth a thousand times its value" (SN 1.107)

The Buddha said that *dana* ranked alongside Truth, self-control and patience in terms of its importance for humanity. In his typical free spirited way, the Buddha urged Upali, a follower of the Buddha, to give *dana* to the believers to the Jains. The Buddha regarded the act of giving as so significant that it included giving to those following a religious view with which the Buddha did not feel comfortable. (M.1.371) When rumours went around that the Buddha expected *dana* to go only to him, he told people that they should give *dana* to those they 'have confidence in,' to those of 'upright character.' He clearly regarded the Jain leader and his monks of upright character. The Buddha sets down an important principle of knowing the character of the person (s) when we give recipient(s) whether we offer our services, time or money.

Countless numbers of people engage in acts of service to gurus, spiritual teachers and leaders in the public and private sector. Such people might:

- arrange
- clean
- promote
- manage
- organise
- cook
- keep accounts
- and much more.

This serves gives support for leaders of their programmes, workshops and retreats, both residential and non-residential. Supporters might offer their homes as a place for the teacher/workshop leader to stay. Various forms of service from a supporter requires personal sacrifice, dedication and a commitment before a programme gets underway, during the programme and then attention to all the closing details.

Far too many people, who give their time and love for events, find themselves taken for granted. They might receive barely a word of thanks. Without the commitment of such individuals, these events would never take place. These servants of various teachings are often referred to in the East, and in some Western traditions, as karma yogis: yogis of action.

Engaged in putting on a programme, the karma yogis, who are may receive a stipend, a donation for their services or freely offer their services. Genuine expressions of appreciation and gratitude towards karma yogis matter. A real 'THANK YOU" has power to it. It is a statement of gratitude, a recognition of the kindness and dedication of supporters. The leader needs to show that he or she recognises the various acts of love of the karma yogi, and expresses appreciation, personally and publicly. This is a small gift of love from the leader to those who enable the leader to teach.

Some karma yogis find fault with themselves rather than ask the leader why he or she takes them for granted. "It must be my ego looking for praise" a karma yogi might wrongly assume. There is a difference between the natural wish for appreciation and the desire for praise. The desire for praise reflects a blind spot in the inner life when a person receives a real appreciation and gratitude and yet it is not enough – it does not fill the empty space within.

We cannot satisfy the thirst for praise which exists on the other side of the coin to blame. People work best together in an atmosphere of love, of generosity and mutual support. If the leader takes his or her supporters for granted, they will become disillusioned and drift away. If the leader does not walk the talk, then the karma yogis will also talk with their feet.

The Significance of Intention

The Buddha praised those who provide a facility -"a Dharma residence (community, centre, monastery, hermitage) *as giving a great deal*" but regarded "*the greatest gift of all as the teaching of the* Dharma *and giving of knowledge and understanding of the Deathless.*" (SN.121).

On several occasions, the Buddha used the concept Deathless referring to a realizable liberation not limited by birth and death. In his teachings of the gradual path to full awakening, he would often begin with the significance of the act of giving as the first step to liberation, followed by the virtues of non-harming, non-exploitation and then inner development through mindfulness and meditation on to the full exploration of daily life. He encouraged clarity of mind in the intention behind the act of giving as well as recognition of the possible consequences. In the Dharma, giving is not for giving's sake but includes mindfulness of intention, action and result. The whole process from initiative to consequences matters.

I recall in the 1980's leading a regular men's group in Totnes, England my home town. I had heard that a local women's group in the town had agreed to take some of their jewelry to Dartmoor, a large national park, 45 minutes' drive away, and engage in a small ceremony together to return some of their items of jewelry to the earth. Inspired with this

76

initiative, I suggested to the men's group that the next time we met we bring with us an item to give away as a *dana:* an item that we would not normally wish to give away.

Mother Theresa of Calcutta once said to me "Giving only starts when it is difficult to give." I had no sooner made this suggestion to the group than I knew that I would have to give away a favourite Buddhist book that had been with me for 20 years. It was not as if it was the only copy, I did have a more recent edition, but my well-thumbed book had travelled with me for years in the East and afterwards. I tried to tell myself to give another item away but I knew it would be avoidance. After all in the scheme of things, it was a very small gesture.

Authentic *dana* pushes us beyond the comfort zone, not to make a martyr of ourselves but to understand that giving and letting go reveal the same event. When the men's group met, I placed the book on the table along with the other gifts from the other men. We then chose one of the gifts from the pile. We all knew that each item meant something personal to one of us. We probably all felt a little discomfort with the loss of a treasured item but we shared our happiness at the opportunity to make another man happy with our gift. It is easy to give on an occasional basis. There are 108 (a number indicating infinity in the Buddhist tradition) ways to give just as there are 108 ways to meditate.

Dana serves as a truly challenging practice. The Buddha said that the gift of Dharma, the gift of Truth, excels all other gifts (Dp.354) since it awakens us to reality. *Dana* functions as the opponent force to greed, selfishness and possessiveness that remains dependent on the whole construct of "I" "me", and "mine." The miserly minded person resists sharing and holds back from offering authentic generosity, so remains closed hearted. More will be asked of those that give. The practice of generosity serves as a vehicle

77

for transformation from getting to giving while knowing the worthwhile nature of the gift. The Buddha said the rich person who keeps his wealth to himself digs his own grave (Sn 102).

The most loved individuals in human history have given much, sometimes their life. Such noble ones continue to inspire others to give, regardless of the risks. The Buddha (MN I 447) commented: "Just as seeds sown in fertile well-watered fields yield beautiful crops so those who give themselves to spiritual practice yield great results (such as joy, love and awakening). The giver may not ever know the far-reaching impact of what he or she gives. There is no way to measure the noble act of generosity and the dedication to selfless expressions.

A young woman came to me in some distress. She had ended a relationship she had been in for several years. Then, her former partner had attended the same retreat as herself and their feelings for each other sparked during the retreat. Afterwards they went to a hotel and made love. Within a matter of weeks, she found herself pregnant and alone. She had intended to go on long retreats in the East, perhaps take ordination as a nun, but now her future depended upon her decision. Could she face being a single mother in a European country with little opportunity to attend Dharma retreats? We spoke about the matter together and inquired into her deepest thoughts, feelings and intentions. A few days later, she contacted me and told me she had rejected an abortion and would have trust in the way her life unfolded.

She told me, "Life is a *dana*. Life is a gift to us out of the nature of things. I must treat the pregnancy as a gift. For the first time, I have really understood the meaning of *dana* and why the Buddha gave it such eminence in his teachings."

I saw the woman and her daughter a few years later. She said: "Even though I find being a single mother very difficult and very challenging, I am so happy I kept trust with the gift of life. My daughter is the greatest gift I ever received."

Application of *dana* in Buddhist countries

The tradition of *dana* (the act of generosity, the practice of giving), has made a lasting impression in the hearts of many of us who have travelled to the East, to Buddhist countries, and the sub-continent of India. We have experienced, for ourselves, the immeasurable devotion and support for the monasteries and ashrams by laypeople. Monks, nuns and laypeople in Buddhist countries treated Westerners, upon arrival at a monastery, with the utmost kindness and respect. They have provided us not only with teachings but also with a hut, meals and all the necessary requisites. We could stay as long as we wished whether as a layperson or whether we took ordination at a later date. No mention of payment arose. The Abbot, monks and nuns did not require any reimbursement for the length of stay. The ordained and local supporters encouraged Western practitioners to stay indefinitely, without any expectation for payment to cover costs in supporting Western guests.

There are few parallel models of such selfless *dana*, especially in the West. We didn't book a room or hut or send advance payment. We were not asked to pay a daily rate. In our naivety, we were more likely to take such acts of generosity and hospitality for granted. We could not speak the language of the Buddhist country, had no knowledge of the religious traditions and culture and made numerous errors as a result, yet continued to be treated as honoured guests. We lived on little money and avoided hotels. Our hosts in the Buddhist monasteries could tell by our appearance that we carried very little in the way of money. It was not as if they thought they would get some large *dana* from us at the end of our stay.

I remember I stayed for three weeks in the forest monastery of Ajahn Buddhadasa in Chai Ya, southern Thailand. At the end of my first visit, I had the wish to give the monastery some modest payment as a guest. I approached Ajahn Poh, the second monk in charge of the monastery to ask him what would be an appropriate donation. "Whatever you wish" he replied in a very nonchalant way. I coaxed him further. He quietly and unassumingly suggested that I go to the morning market in Chai Ya to buy a couple of kilos of bananas (the cheapest fruit) to offer the Abbot and monks. More than 60 monks lived in the forest monastery at that time. A couple of kilos of bananas for nearly three weeks stay! Such a small incident touched in me a deep place of appreciation for the generous hospitality of the monastery and the Buddhist tradition of *dana*.

Many other Westerners who stayed in Buddhist monasteries share similar stories. People in rural Buddhist countries often struggle to make ends meet. They are dependent on the climate, sound economic management from central government and freedom from corruption, nationally and locally. We, the Western guests, wondered whether, upon return to the West, we could possibly find the same inspiration to make the Dharma available to others, while keeping the spirit and letter of *dana* alive regardless of a person's financial circumstances. It has not been easy, and at times it has proved to be an uphill struggle.

At first glance, it should be easier in the West to establish the practice of generosity (*dana*) than in the East. Although there is poverty and hardship in the West, and a mountain of debts, Western Buddhists and practitioners are much better off, generally speaking, than many of their Asian counterparts. As the Dharma makes the journey from East to

West, the dialogue around Dharma and *dana* became an important platform to make the teachings available to as many people as possible. It has been a challenging task in the West, with its countless shadows of anxiety around money and the future inhibiting the full commitment to *dana* that belongs to the tradition of Dharma service.

Since the world becomes enslaved through desire and market forces, *dana* encourages a radical engagement with society by endorsing a direct alternative to the buying and selling of services. The Buddha said acts of giving (*dana*) are "like a rain cloud drenching the Earth with showers of gifts."

Dharma teachings give rise to *dana* and *dana* gives rise to Dharma. *Dana* challenges the contemporary view that human beings must engage in a financial transaction for all forms of personal guidance, knowledge and inner development if the service has real value. With this view, the more we pay, the more we believe in what is on offer. Enshrined in the political/economic thinking of our time, the view that treats services as a product, buckles when faced with the teachings and application of *dana*. Living in direct accordance with empathy (*anukampa*) with the Dharma, we experience a generosity that triggers support for the development of humanity through solicited and unsolicited acts of *giving*. The Buddha said there are several blessings for individuals (or organisations and centres) who offer *dana*:

- *a long life,*
- *appreciation of many,*
- *noble association,*
- *beautiful reputation,*
- *confidence,*
- *ethics, mental development and dana constitutes action with real merit to it. (A.V.34).*

Dana in the West

We need to remind ourselves of these blessings. The faith of Buddhists in Asia enables wonderful acts of selfless support for the monasteries. Staff at various Western centres also makes genuine personal sacrifices to enable a centre to run. In many centers, the staff receives a very modest monthly stipend enabling a centre to keep the costs of the daily rate for retreatants as affordable as possible. The daily rate would be significantly higher if every member of staff received a salary, even the minimum hourly wage. The staff gives service as a *dana*. The boards of directors and trustees also give *dana* through their service. Upon this basis of application of time and energy wherever possible, Dharma centres have grown significantly over the years. To take one example, the number of centres and Buddhist groups in Germany quadrupled during the 1990's. Without love of the Dharma-*dana*, this would never have happened.

Buddhist monks and nuns rely totally on *dana* and there are a small number of Dharma teachers who also depend totally on similar support. Other teachers also earn income through writing Dharma books, counselling, pension, investments or through the benefit of a personal inheritance. Some teachers barely receive enough *dana* to pay taxes. Their love of Dharma comes before their personal considerations.

This remarkable tradition of *dana* deserves an unwavering commitment from the whole Sangha so that we revere *dana* as an indispensable feature of the tradition. There is a growing disquiet at the systematic escalation of costs of retreats, especially in the USA, that may seriously undermine the principle of *dana* and the commitment to making retreats truly affordable. The Buddha encouraged a life founded on *danapatthani*: a life with a 'foundation of giving.' Although people in a profession may not bat an eyelid at the cost of retreats, a growing number of dedicated Dharma practitioners and young people with little in the way of income, feel differently.

Young people, students, single parents, the unemployed and homeless, wandering yogis, those on low income, elderly people living on a state pension or modest savings and those in debt deserve equally easy access to Dharma retreats, workshops and public talks. There is an understandable resistance among many of those struggling to make ends meet, to appeal to a centre for financial assistance. Yogis are not fond of the "cap in hand" mentality when making contact with a centre for financial aid as they feel like beggars.

We bring from the East the Buddhist tradition's love of *dana* that offers teachings and practices outside the secular system. No one would say it is an easy methodology. At every retreat and every workshop, the teacher or a manager has to explain the *dana* as practice, and the reliance of teachers and sometimes staff on receiving *dana*. The message goes out at the end of the event with a *dana* bowl for teachers, a bowl for staff and a bowl to support the centre. Some yogis have listened to numerous *dana* talks, usually lasting five to 10 minutes, on numerous occasions. They could probably recite them backwards. In the meditation hall, other yogis, who have never been to an Asian monastery, never heard the concept of *dana* before, will listen to the short explanation for the first time. Some imagine that the appeal for *dana* is a tip for teachers, an opportunity to buy a slice of carrot cake with a cafe latte rather than support for all the daily necessities! It is the responsibility of those who receive *dana* to use the gift wisely and prudently to support the basic needs of food, clothing, household expenses and medicine.

The Sangha often supports teachers and organisers on *dana*. This makes it possible for teachers to teach full time and engage in various forms of Dharma service in daily life. The willingness of the Sangha to dig deeply into their pockets to support teachers, staff and centres, generates incredible levels of gratitude and appreciation from the beneficiaries.

The act of the gift gives the giver the touch of a sweet happiness, more subtle than the gaining of any pleasure through the senses. At times, an act of generosity, a personal sacrifice on behalf of others challenges one's peace of mind, while knowing that one is staying true to the universal principle of giving. Life is given to us and life is taken away. Nothing remains for us to hold onto in the transitions between life and death. The offerings of today make the transitions of life to death an easier process because the practice of giving shows a practice of letting go. In the last period of our short life on earth, our practices of giving, of letting go, will contribute to letting go of any clinging to life so that we can make the transition from life to death without stress or fear.

The capacity to give and receive ensures the free movement of life through an accord of mutual understanding and respect. Giving and receiving confirms the great gestures of life, a sign of compassion, free from the burden of wanting more from the event. There is no greater power of the heart than to give.

Life is given to us through the nature of things. To give is to abide in accordance with the unfoldment of life. The freedom to give wisely confirms one of the true transformations of the inner life.

Chapter Five

Spirituality for Lovers

Acts of loving kindness are a memorable quality that creates love and respect and is conducive to unity. MN 104.21

A life of distorted perceptions and values impacts upon a personal, social and global life. The unhealthy deeds of taking, of removing, of having for oneself will take priority over the act of giving. In the epic Sanskrit play, the *Ramayana*, Rama and Sita gave up the comforts of their palace in Ayodhya to go into exile in the forests of Dandakaranya. The King Ravana's sister fell in love with Rama. She made repeated attempts to persuade Rama to leave Sita and come to live with her. Then Ravana, obsessed with Sita, kidnapped her through showing her a golden deer to impress her. Ravana held Sita captive in Sri Lanka and tried to win her over, but she never wavered in her love for Rama. Her husband searched for her, and eventually defeated Ravana and rescued Sita.

The Buddha warned incessantly of the suffering that entails when we take that which has not been given and Sita had not made a commitment to Ravana. The story demonstrates the insensitive heart and the cold mind when we deprive another of their freedom, and their heart's connection with somebody else. Sita loved Rama not Ravana. A wise relationship shows itself as expressions of love.

After the rescue, Rama seriously doubted whether Sita still loved him and had remained faithful to him. It is the story of a man's great quest for the renewal of love, overcoming of all the obstacles, and a triumph of love over adversity. Yet the *Ramayana* reminds us that doubts can still haunt the mind. This longing for union gains a metaphysical

85

status thus retold in stories, poetry, art and plays. The pursuit of union of oneself with another reveals the power of longing often found in the greatest stories ever told. Union with another then becomes a priority. Oneness with another also exposes the times of being apart from another with the opportunity to appreciate aloneness; otherwise the inner life reacts with loneliness, sometimes sliding into despair. Rama loved Sita in her absence and presence, but also experienced the torments of doubt about her love for him.

True love can enter consciousness at any point in time, while Dharma wisdom and Eros can knit together in the same way as Dharma and solitude easily connect.

Naivety and projections result in the idealisation of the object of our love. In the midst of powerful sensations of romantic love, the one who falls in love finds it hard to see any shortcomings in the other. The virtues, the love and the presence of another nourish every region of the heart. There are no perceptions of the limitations or faults of the other. It is not necessary to look for these flaws. In the passage of time, they will emerge to enable love to have a depth and breadth that includes the human frailties of the other. Romantic and creative love needs to develop the capacity to embrace the whole person. When two people fall in love with each other, they often share a language from the depths of their being.

- *"I feel I have known you for a long, long time."*
- *"We are made for each other."*
- *"I felt we were one from the very beginning."*
- *"It is truly divine when we are together."*

Lovers say such words with real meaning and conviction, not as throwaway remarks. Such love reveals a sense of fulfilment, a deep connection, a sharing of the Truth of one's experience in communion with another. In the merging of one's love with another's love, the divine and inner fulfilment meet together. Both lovers reciprocate their love for each other. Romantic love benefits both parties. In this exalted state, wondrous experiences and immeasurable acts of love shake up the inhibitions of the self. Love flows in two directions becoming more real than death – and thus pointing to the deathless, namely that discovery of a freedom without beginning or end.

The experience of such love reveals its vulnerability to change, to shifts in perception due to shaping of views over the course of time. These changes in view and feelings should not inhibit us from falling totally in love. Such deep love is too important to undermine as it is a divine element of human existence. Romantic love belongs to an expression of *metta*, a divine abiding.

Deep nourishment comes from romantic love. It doesn't deny the challenges that accompany such experiences, sooner or later. The charge, the power and presence of Eros between two people or from one person to another (even without reciprocation) opens out the heart to a deep discovery of intimacy. Outsiders often dwell on the differences between two people, differences such as age, power, knowledge, class, wealth, life experience and beauty. They fail to understand the intensity of romance between two people.

The intensely romantic story of Krishna and Radha in their home town of Vrindavan, serves as a symbol of the power of love between a man and a woman. Krishna had many women around him who loved his presence, his playfulness and his wisdom. Despite being married to someone else, Radha felt an overwhelmingly rapturous love for Krishna, born from a single glance between them. In a single moment, both Krishna and Radha entered into a profound state of romantic love. Even though Krishna travelled to teach in parts of North India, and serve as the charioteer for Arjuna in the great battle between two families, Radha and Krishna's love and devotion to each other remained undiminished and unaffected by time and space, absence and distance. Their story points to a divine abiding for Krishna and Radha. Krishna fused their divine energy together.

The movement of love can move back and forth between two people in ways that other people cannot comprehend. For example, outsiders may have made up their mind about a power imbalance in a partnership without even spending real time with the two people concerned. Or women may feel patronised and discriminated against when outsiders tell them they hold an inferior position in a relationship. Appearances may not reveal reality. True love has a power that addresses and accommodates immense differences between two people.

Mutually shared love between Krishna and Radha love reveals a beautiful connection, as well as the capacity to accommodate any power differential between them. People revered Krishna as a god while Radha looked upon him in that way too. Krishna, the god, and Radha, the married woman, had the inner power to make known their love for each other, despite the taboos of the time: a god and a woman in love, yet the woman was betrothed elsewhere.

Fear of intimacy inhibits natural expressions of romantic love. Romantic love pours into consciousness but then fear of commitment arises. Others have a fear of not finding intimacy. The desire for union then takes priority in the inner life over love of aloneness, of the solitary way. An imbalance in power places one person over and above the other. This may lead to a desire for autonomy for the one who is feeling in the shadow of the other. This is likely to end in an argument, if not in tears. If oppressed by another, if one voice does not count, he or she feels helpless and undervalued. This helplessness acts as the breeding ground for doubts, even smouldering resentment. The one who has more power and authority in other areas of daily life must remain vigilant in their personal life, otherwise a relationship will fall apart. Nevertheless, 'tis better to have loved and lost than never to have loved at all' as the poet Alfred Tennyson said. Yes, romantic love sometimes obscures wise judgement. If a relationship disintegrates, the two people may have to endure the "I told you so" voices, but love never offers guarantees. That's what makes being in love such an adventure.

The Buddha treated togetherness and separation as two forms of experience to know and understand. The Dharma's priority on love and wisdom, rather than union of the self with the other, contributes to an authentic emotional development to handle change: to appreciate intimacy and appreciate aloneness. Awakening embraces aloneness and togetherness free from dependency on union, free from the anguish of separation.

I have compiled *25 Practices in a Relationship* drawn upon many years of experience in relationships.

25 Practices in a Relationship

1.   *A true relationship is a pillar of real support. Such a relationship makes the two people powerful in the best sense. Their relationship encourages fearlessness and loving acts in the world.*

2.   *Acknowledge acts of love in more ways than words. Love is also mindful presence, taking care of the children, the home, garden, acts of generosity, dialogue and letting go. Reflect on the forms of love you offer and the forms of love you receive. They may be different.*

3.   At times, we need to apologise for acts of our body, speech and mind. Make sure that your apology is sincere. Express a genuine regret at a time when you can make eye contact. Do not imagine you can keep on bringing up the feeling of regret or remorse, no matter what you did or did not do. Do not expect that your partner can keep expressing heartfelt remorse as time passes by.

4.   Be flexible. A relationship moves between the divine realm of a god and goddess being together and the human realm of friendship and ordinary life. Both are important.

5.   Be kind. Kindness is powerful. Kindness connects and heals.

6.   Be mindful of the feelings, needs and history of the partner.

7.   Because two people have been together for years, it does not indicate they have a depth of love and intimacy. Do not assume they know anything about being in a relationship. Never underestimate habit, insecurity and fear of change in keeping a relationship together. Because a relationship does not last a long time, it does not mean the two people did not experience a depth of love and intimacy. Because a person is a practising celibate, it does not mean he or she knows nothing about an intimate relationship.

8.   Blame is the virus that destroys love as much as AIDS destroys the body. Don't confuse honesty with negativity.

9.   *Don't bring up hurts that are more than a week old unless you want to go on feeling sorry for yourself and wear your partner out.*

10.   *Don't destroy love by rubbishing members of your partner's family or his or her relationship to them. After all, he or she couldn't choose their family member, but did choose you!*

11.   *If someone is complaining to you about their partner, remember it is half the story. Do not just agree with what you hear. Do not automatically take sides. Ask questions. Don't feed their reactivity.*

12.   *If you forgive, then state it and afterwards keep the lips sealed and don't bring up the issue again. It is like putting a dirty finger into a wound expecting it to heal.*

13.   *If your partner does something irresponsible or uncaring, don't keep pressing him or her for an explanation. It is unlikely any reason will seem satisfactory. The 'offending' partner may not be able to explain to himself/herself what he or she did, let alone to you.*

14.   *If your partner has a responsible role of any kind, then try to understand the pressures that go with the role. If your partner has no primary role at work or home, then try to understand how important the relationship will be.*

15.   *Know deeply the difference between love and desire.*

16.   *Let go of the idea of working on your relationship. We work enough already. Don't cling to ideals about a relationship. Instead, ask within. "What is love? What way can I express it today?"*

17.   Love matters. Whether you are in a relationship or not is incidental. Do not believe yourself when you tell yourself that you can work better on yourself in a relationship or outside of one. That belief is based on the current interests of the 'self.' Love is the issue.

18.   Never believe you can change someone. You can point things out endlessly and eventually your critical remarks or outbursts will become destructive. The faultfinder will only see the faults and the receiver of the critical remarks will inwardly withdraw or return the fire.

19.   Never undermine your partner's vision or their roles. If you do, your partner will be reluctant to share their roles and vision with you.

20.   Regard the relationship as a powerful force for diving deep inside finding the Truth in the situation and realisation that self and other consists of constructions of feelings and views. In Truth, there is neither togetherness, nor separation, neither sameness nor differences.

21.   Take no notice of ordained Buddhists and religions who say that you have to have desire to make love. You need love to make love. Desire is a completely different formation, produces different sensations, different thoughts and stifles the erotic. Lovemaking is erotic. Desire is self-interest. Love allows passion to flow freely while desire produces tension and agitation. Make love! In bed. In the bath. Under the table. Under the stars. Anywhere. No matter what your age.

22.   Take total responsibility for everything that you feel. This is a sign of maturity. Be mindful of the words that follow the word "You..." when speaking to your partner. The relationship lives and dies on what follows from the word "You...."

23.   *Talk. Love reveals itself most easily in the sheer enjoyment of two partners talking to each other and both feeling understood. When two people love talking to each other, love also being together when they say little or nothing, they truly love each other.*

24.   *The claim 'I have made so many sacrifices for you in this relationship' is an ego trip. It is a confirmation of resentment at not getting what one wants from one's partner. Then you will want your partner to pay for your sacrifice. A sacrifice ceases to be a sacrifice when you want something in return.*

25.   *When a relationship is over, it is often just as hard for the one who ends the relationship as for the one on the receiving end. The one who ends it may have to deal with deep regret later for terminating the relationship and cutting the other person out of their life. Wisdom can make the transition from partners to friends.*

You may keep lovingly to all the above tips but never for a day stop your practice of impermanence (*anicca*)! Never take your partner for granted. Life brings together and life takes apart. A relationship relies on many factors, known and unknown. It is important to remember that the quality of time together matters more than the quantity of time together. The Buddha's emphasis on the application of a mindful presence in meditation and to daily tasks, also equally applies in relationship. Mindful presence contributes to finding out more and more about the other person through the years. Nobody stands still. Nobody remains the same. Love keeps a relationship alive. Love is mindful presence with interest.

The Buddha said: *"Just as if a mighty trumpeter were with little difficulty to make proclamation to the four directions (upwards, downwards, across, everywhere), so by this meditation, by this liberation of the heart through love (metta), he or she leaves nothing untouched, nothing unaffected, without ill will."* (DN 13.77)

It is far too easy for two people to grasp onto views about each other as if the views had some inherent Truth to them. The mind easily forms its conceit out of notions of superiority, inferiority or equality. There is no real Truth in any of these perceptions. As long as the dynamic of change emerges out of the multiple conditions, it would be foolish to pursue a goal of equality in the ups and downs of daily life. The principle of enquiry particularly applies to suffering with the tendency to put down oneself (inferiority), blame another (oneself as superior) or conclude that both are at fault (equality). These measurements may continue in the short or long term as long as they go unexamined.

Who and what can cause suffering? We make various claims:

1. *I make my own suffering*
2. *Others bring suffering upon me*
3. *We bring suffering on each other*
4. *Various circumstances (accident, redundancy, climate change) outside of the two people cause our suffering.*

If I create my own suffering, then my suffering would not depend on anyone else or anything else. Why on earth would any mildly sane person want to create their own suffering? Who am I that I would want to do that to my 'self.' How can I separate myself from the suffering that I bring upon myself? Such a view can generate more unhappiness, guilt, self-blame and suicidal thoughts.

I may think that somebody else causes all my suffering. If another has the power to cause us to suffer, then we can never get away from the suffering that others inflict upon us. Others would always have the power to cause us suffering. Such a view can generate anger, revenge, attack on another and/or the identification of being a victim.

If both of us caused the suffering we go through together, then what part of us caused suffering and what part did not? Why do we allow one part of each other to cause each other suffering when there is another part inside us that does not cause suffering?

If suffering arose due to circumstances outside of each other, then we can never be free from suffering. We would suffer due to fate, accidents, destiny, evolution, nature or the hand of God. There is no need to point the accusing finger at ourselves, another, or both, or to circumstances outside of ourselves and another. If we do this, then we can then respond with wisdom to the arising of suffering.

We have the capacity to end the arising of suffering. Love replaces suffering. Mindfulness and equanimity replaces suffering. Letting go replaces suffering. Ending of healthy views transforms suffering. Clear comprehension and understanding of causuality dissolves suffering.

Let us explore the resources, inwardly and with others, to dissolve the whole mass of stress, anguish and fear, once and for all. Let love and wisdom pervade consciousness.

Chapter 6

Can a Spiritual Teacher be a Close Friend?

The Buddha said: "If one can find a worthy friend, then walk with him content and mindful." MN 128.

Relationships develop through neither adhering to a notion of hierarchy nor adherence to a notion of equality. If we constantly place another above ourselves, we will consistently experience a submissive relationship. Even though resentment may well build inside ourselves, our fears inhibit us from speaking up in case we find ourselves subjected to disapproval, outright rejection or humiliation. Yet, certain people close to us or at a distance may be far more knowledgeable. We can learn from that person. The same person may be poorly equipped in other matters or aspects of the same subject. Perhaps we know and understand more so that our voice of authority takes precedence at that time.

It can work the other way around, too. We are the voice of authority on certain matters but there may well be a gap, sometimes a very large gap, in terms of our knowledge, skills, insights and application. We need to be confident in what we know and be free from arrogance. Arrogance preserves the hierarchy. We equally need the humility to know that even full awakening; complete enlightenment does not mean omniscience or anything even nearly approaching omniscience. The Buddha rubbished teachers who claimed to be all knowing and had planted themselves on the top of the hierarchy – religious, spiritual or political.

We can believe in the basic equality between people while still having respect for others and be willing to learn from them. We need to realise and appreciate how much we all have in common. Attachment to a hierarchy can feed the ego of superiority and inferiority, the controller and the controlled. There are differences between people but we do not have to grasp onto these differences to feed our ego on being either superior or inferior. Through recognizing differences between people, we can develop wisdom and compassion. Friendship contributes to the dissolution of problems between people and our perceptions of each other.

In the world of spiritual authority, gurus, imams, priests, rabbis and spiritual masters generally remain aloof from their followers. This kind of authority figure does not share his or her personal life with their Dharma students, (followers, disciples or parishioners) nor socialise with them. The figure will appear in various settings to offer teachings and then withdraw. It is the same in the professional life. Generally, patients do not socialise with their doctor, students with their teacher or a clients with their psychotherapist. The conventional view observes a strict boundary so that the respective role remains while excluding friendship. This approach sets clear guidelines for forms of behaviour and communication.

It is clear from the widespread teachings of the Buddha that he did not adopt the professional or religious model of relationship such as the psychotherapist or priest. He stated that the Dharma teacher acts as a spiritual friend (*kalyana mitta*) as well as an authority figure since the teacher belongs to the Sangha of practitioners. The *kalyana mitta* has an indispensable function in the Buddha's teachings. The dynamic and exploratory nature of the Sangha, including the voices of authority, moves outside of the religious and professional criteria and points to the full exploration of deep friendship (with all the risks and potential misunderstanding that can arise between teachers and Dharma students).

Some Dharma teachers have very little social contact with their students. They teach retreats, offer workshops, give

97

public talks, and perhaps attend retreat centre committee meetings. Outside of these functions as a teacher, they may well disappear from public view. They withdraw into their homes from personal contact and association with the Sangha. Some teachers find this necessary in order to renew their energy as well as find time to prepare talks or write books, although at the cost of informal contact with the Sangha.

Some Dharma teachers avoid developing friendships within the Sangha. A teacher's close friendship with the Sangha, inside and out of retreats, does not make him 'one of the boys or girls,' so to speak. The teachers must know themselves, their position of authority, and be willing to voice it any time.

We can develop deep and lasting friendships in the Sangha through living as a body of spiritual friends while acknowledging the variety of roles. The teacher who regularly meets with Dharma students in various environments will get to know the students far more than in the formality of a retreat. Of course, a powerful presence of a teacher may diminish through yogis (commonly used to mean Dharma students) seeing the Dharma teacher as a friend. The students who spend informal time with their teacher will learn a lot about their teacher and may find out things about him or her and their lifestyle that may affect their perception. But that is what Sangha explores – the dynamics of "self" and "other."

Dharma teachers frequently bring in stories and experiences into their teachings. Priests, rabbis, doctors, schoolteachers, psychologists and others in similar helping professions very rarely share a story from their personal life with their parishioners, clients or patients. They maintain a professional boundary between themselves and those they serve.

It requires skillful application of several factors of the Noble Eightfold Path to secure and develop deep friendship.

If unclear, teacher and yogis will probably slip into painful projections and fantasy in contact with another that lead to vulnerable feelings. The development of *kalyana mitta* can generate a liberating wisdom or, through unresolved needs, produce a cesspit of confusion and misunderstanding. Seniors in the Dharma, directors of centres, retreat managers and long-standing experienced yogis, and those taking their first steps into the way of Dharma, need regular contact to develop a collective trust.

Teachers, trustees and directors can make errors of judgment inside and outside of retreats. Mistakes can occur. Either the authority figure or the practitioner may misunderstand the other's intentions or their own.

These are conservative times. There continues to be a considerable and understandable reaction to the permissive attitudes of a generation ago, particularly in relation to issues around sex. This has had a significant impact on contemporary Dharma teachers, young and old, as well as the rest of the Sangha. There is also the problem of idealizing projections from the students, along with teachers grasping onto their role and power. There have been various allegations, ranging from flirtatious behaviour to romantic involvement and sexual intimacy between teachers and yogis. Some in the Sangha see suspension or banishment of a teacher, as a responsible way to ensure a climate of safety. Others, teachers and yogis, see the same decision as a vindictive and unnecessary punishment of a teacher for developing a relationship with a practitioner.

There is a widespread view that it is not possible for a person to fulfill two roles with the same person - a professional and personal relationship. Those who hold to this standpoint demand the separation of one role from the other. But the role of authority and personal friendship can work together in the Sangha. In an authentic relationship, there is a meeting without the unconscious projections that distort perceptions.

In the Buddhist tradition, the violation of the third precept "*kamesu micchacara*" is generally translated as *sexual misconduct*. This set a limitation to the Buddha's use of *kamesu micchacara*. The Pali gives the concept a much wider meaning: *Kamesu micchacara* refers to "*misconduct through sense-pleasure.*" This certainly includes forms of sexually harmful behaviour but equally includes any harmful, excessive and mindless stimulation through all of the senses: eyes, ears, nose, tongue, touch or inwardly. It is very convenient to define the third precept exclusively around sexuality as it would enable the Sangha to ignore the wider implications of this precept. Practitioners would perhaps then question the lifestyle of a teacher, as well as themselves, if it is not in accordance with moderation and sustainability.

A Question of Trust

In Ancient Greece, the philosophers placed friendship at the heart of a fulfilled life. Plato said that Socrates viewed a close friendship as more significant than possession of all the gold. Epicurus wrote that friendship and wisdom were the two goals of life. Aristotle wrote that friendship goes towards the whole of the person not just to "incidental details." The word "idiot" comes from the Greek "idiotes" – it means "one who only lives for themselves." As a divine virtue, friendship belongs to the very heart of Dharma practice, interlocking with wisdom and liberation.

The Buddha commented: "*Not the sweet smell of flowers, not even the fragrance of jasmine, blow against the wind. But the fragrance of virtuous people pervades all directions.*" (Dh 54).

The Sangha must remain committed to the ongoing practice of virtue, as well as training in meditation and living with wisdom. Dharma teachers and other practitioners need to ensure development of the spiritual friend (*kalyana mitta*) for all who take refuge in the Sangha. I believe it is not necessary for teachers to isolate themselves from the Sangha outside of teaching venues.

During the 1980's, various Buddhist teachers first met their wives, husbands or partners while teaching a retreat. A generation later some of the same teachers disapprove of other teachers and younger teachers developing a similar contact with a meditator after a retreat.

In an early year of this century, I attended a meeting of Dharma teachers at the Spirit Rock Centre in California. The two facilitators from the Zen tradition gave us outlines on paper dealing with the issue of Dharma teachers and retreat participants, often referred to as yogis. One page was headed "Possible Dharma teacher involvement with students." We were handed papers for our consideration that referred to:

- *no special friendships*
- *a Dharma teacher does not go out for dinner or a movie with students*
- *attend only* Sangha *business meetings in student homes*
- *jealousy is possible or likely and making things "even" is difficult*
- *no dual role*
- *no romantic or special relationships*
- *one cannot be a special friend and also a* Dharma *teacher for the same person*
- *avoid too much presence in the person's life*
- *professional relationship must be terminated before a romantic relationship is pursued*

- *potential for harm and suffering between the teacher and the Dharma student*

There is a widespread view that there is an inherent abuse of trust if a close or intimate friendship arises between teachers and Dharma students. Most teachers at the meeting agreed that if a romantic or personal relationship seems to be on the horizon, the teacher should tell his or her student to find another teacher in order to safeguard any conflict of interest with regard to the dual role of teacher and friend/partner. They adopted the view that it is wrong to support a dual role because it will lead to confusion and conflict. I would agree with the risks but there is equally the potential for a close empathy, deep friendship and insight through both roles. It takes mindfulness and clear comprehension to know the potential and to know desire for the sensual or the mixture of both.

The teacher/practitioner relationship is asymmetrical and this means the teacher has the responsibility to recognise any transference or projections upon him or her from the student and his or her own counter transference towards the students, otherwise confusion develops for both at the expense of clear communication. Dharma practice includes seeing through the transference and projections onto another.

Conservative Buddhist teachers say that the power imbalance between the teacher and yogi leaves the yogi vulnerable. They claim that the teacher, as an authority figure, would take advantage of the vulnerability of the yogi. They will oppose the view that meaningful consent, based on contextual circumstances and shared responsibility, can arise between two adults. Not all teachers and yogis agree with this assumption. Some dedicated practitioners have told me that Buddhist institutions have no business interfering with the development of friendship and intimacy within the Sangha.

These yogis, women and men, categorically reject the standpoint that they are vulnerable, easily manipulated and caught up in problematic transference onto a Dharma teacher. They dispute the notion that they are blindly susceptible to the attentions of a teacher and cannot handle a dual role of intimacy (sexual or otherwise) and still attend the retreats offered by the teacher. The tradition of *kalayana mitta* supports the development of friendship and the capacity for the individual to act with integrity towards another. Foolishness may arise. I believe a code of morality that blocks informal communication anywhere, and at any time, is not the solution.

A practitioner in her 20's showed the potential to become a Dharma teacher. The young teacher joined some workshops to explore sexuality. This caused concern in a Buddhist institution, triggering a discussion at an international Buddhist teachers meeting as to whether or not an ethics committee should be set up of seniors in the Dharma to deal with matters of morality. The young woman wished to explore in groups "mindfulness in sexuality, tools for intimacy and orgasmic meditation." Some of us take the view that the aspiring teacher could benefit considerably from such an exploration, while other Buddhists disapprove of such workshops. To their credit, the group of teachers felt no inclination to form an ethics committee.

There are risks if a senior teacher in the Dharma develops a romantic relationship with a yogi, new or relatively new. The new yogi might feel a sense of betrayal, a loss of trust and doubt in the teachings. Yet stringent rules and attempts to control individuals' feelings and lives exacerbate the problem. With his endorsement of *kalyana mitta*, the Buddha offered a middle ground between a strict professional code and the rejection of all authority. He offered a way of life truly dedicated to spiritual friendship. If we identify with our role as teachers in the same way as a priest or psychiatrist, we will lose sight of the precious significance of *kalyana mitta* for everybody in the Sangha. As Dharma teachers, we are not priests, and we are not professionals.

The *kalyana mitta* does not fall into the same category as a friend or acquaintance in a social sense, namely somebody we hang out with, chat to and engage in superficial levels of communication. In the Sangha, the *kalyana mitta* relationship develops empathy and respect between two or more in the Sangha. There is thoughtful and sensitive use of language free from manipulative intentions. It may occasionally occur that the two people become very close together, as confidants or lovers, but that doesn't necessarily undermine the value of the role of spiritual authority and dedicated practitioner. Wisdom can easily hold dual roles. Inner freedom allows the movement between the two.

The Role of Teachers to the Sangha

Outside of retreats, teachers work in different ways. Some teachers offer one to one Dharma counselling at an hourly rate comparable to psychotherapists. Other teachers offer interviews on a *dana* basis while others simply meet with the yogi without mentioning an hourly rate or *dana*. Some teachers do not offer any kind of personal teaching to a yogi outside of a retreat. It is useful for teachers and the Sangha to review regularly their way of offering the Dharma. Poorer yogis, single parents, elderly people living on a state pension, nomads, India wallahs, unemployed and those in debt can feel excluded from access to the Dharma.

The Buddha criticised teachers who lived a lavish lifestyle, dined out extravagantly, bought expensive clothes and jewelry and led a lifestyle not conducive to the teachings of 'letting go.' *"These teachers were not trained in the way of a sage,"* he said (D 1.105). The Buddha knew the danger of getting out of touch with the reality of most people's lives and the inability to experience deep levels of meditation when the teacher's mind gets consumed in thought around pleasure, money and possessions.

Some teachers will give a lot of personal attention to very wealthy or famous practitioners. After a retreat, they may cultivate a friendship towards a rich meditator with a view towards securing a substantial donation or becoming a spiritual presence in that individual's life. The wealthy student may feel flattered at such attention or feel vulnerable to manipulation. Students of the teacher may make phone calls to the wealthy practitioner to ask him or her if they would like a personal meeting with their teacher. Some wealthy and famous people are sick of being 'cuddled up to' in such a way. Is the teacher engaging with another as a *kalyana mitta* or using his or her role to exploit the good will of the practitioner?

The Buddha teaches us to live a conscious life with supportive teachings and practices. It is well worth reflecting on these lovely quotations below from the Buddha, coming from his heart. We need to take his heartfelt concerns and apply them to our heart. You can feel the kindness and friendship in his words. Every line is worthy of interest, of reflection and meditating upon. If we genuinely applied such kindly advice to ourselves in our daily live, we would develop a genuine peace of mind, happiness with the everyday and a virtuous way of life for our welfare and the welfare of others. At first glance, they appear as simple aphorisms. The transition in the inner life means a genuine movement from a superficial acknowledgement of a verse to developing the capacity to take the lines to heart, to the depth inside, so that an initial aphorism converts into a wise way of life.

Here are a few quotes:

- *"It is natural law that non-remorse will arise in one who is virtuous." (SN 10.2)*

- *"People who only see one side of things engage in quarrels and disputes."*

- *"We will guard the doors of our sense faculties. On seeing a form with the eye, we will not grasp at its signs and features. We will practice the way of restraint." (MN 39)*

- *"It is by living close to a person that his or her virtue is known.*

- *"It is by associating with a person that his or her clarity is known. It is in adversity that a person's fortitude is known. It is by discussion with a person that his or her wisdom is known, and then only after a long period, not a short time." (Ud 6.2).*

- *"Rain soddens what is covered up.*
  It does not sodden what is open
  Therefore uncover what is covered
  Then the rain will not sodden it." (Ud 5.5)

- *For the sake of people struck in the middle of the river, overwhelmed with (approaching) death and decay, there is a solid ground. Sn.193.*

- *If you do not cling to what is in the present, you will dwell calmed. (Sn.949)*

The Power of Empathy

The Buddha made it clear that the *"whole of this spiritual life is lived for spiritual friendship, good companionship and good association"* (SN 45.2) through which we free ourselves from the problematic views around desire, existence and non-existence. Some wish to minimise the differences between the teacher and the student so we treat each other as equals who all share the same Buddha nature.

However, outside of deep realisation, it is not easy to dismiss the powerful and deeply rooted image accompanying important roles. It is in the exchange of the intimacy of the dialogue that liberating realisations can come about. It is not unusual for a student to say: "I felt you were talking directly to me in your teachings this afternoon." He or she is right. The talk should hit the spot for every practitioner with the ears to hear. One of the values of the informal encounter, with its emphasis on intimacy, is the opportunity for role reversal. The student may wish to respond to the teacher with appreciation, insights and helpful feedback. That may well take some time: a time possibly not available during a retreat, and probably not a priority for the student either.

During a retreat, I make an hour available most days for yogis, one after another, to sit next to me at the front of the hall to ask or discuss anything whatsoever. I know from experience that from time to time, a yogi will 'shoot from the hip,' metaphorically speaking. The Buddha said it is the responsibility of Dharma students to point things out to their teacher if they perceive anything unskillful in body, speech and mind from their teacher.

By having a professional outlook on the role of Dharma teacher, along with strict boundaries in terms of contact, teachers may deprive themselves of the opportunity to be the student, to listen and learn from the observations of their students about the activities of their body, speech and mind or likewise the teacher's body, speech and mind.

It takes five minutes to walk from my home in Totnes to the nearby Barrel House coffee shop or Arcturus coffee. I usually go there once a day; sometimes carrying a book or two, or my laptop, or a daily newspaper if something is happening in the world that interests me. I used to sit at a small table by the window downstairs as I enjoy 'people watching' – without having to be responsible for them! Having lived in Totnes since the early 1980's, I have many Dharma friends in the area. I have spent many hours exploring the Dharma of daily life with a person or persons who have joined me at the coffee table. People know where to find me!

I regularly move backwards and forwards between the role of Dharma teacher, yogi, spiritual friend and occasionally guru with those engaging in close personal encounter with me. It is vitally important that the teacher never forgets, not for a single day, that he or she was a Dharma student before being entrusted with the role of Dharma teacher. In the spirit of *kalyana mitta*, we share with the Sangha, privately and publicly, our feelings, experiences and stories connected with our personal relationships, family and social contacts. It is a different responsibility from priests and psychotherapists.

The Sangha of teachers and practitioners explores friendship, shares experiences, supports the practices of each other and contributes to mutual wisdom and liberating knowledge for the welfare of the one and the many.

Chapter 7

Jesus and his Love of the Infinite

Whatever should be done by a compassionate teacher, who, out of compassion, seeks the welfare of his students that I have done for you. AN V11

It is time for Western Buddhists to examine, explore and realise the enlightened teachings of Jesus. It is hair-splitting to make significant differences between the teachings of Jesus and those of the Buddha, especially in matters of love. Jesus continues to be one of the great gods of the Earth who spoke from a place of extraordinary empathy towards people whether family, friends, strangers, rich or poor, religious or otherwise, educated or illiterate. He is a truly exceptional example of the power of love, and occasionally a very tough love, especially concerning social/religious corruption. He challenged unexamined viewpoints, rigidity of tradition and the consequences of egotism and selfishness. He adopted a similar view of the liberating power of divine love as the Buddha. Jesus expressed the importance of love in his teachings whether through story, allegory, similes or heart to heart, mind to mind discourses. On matters of love, the Buddha and Jesus have much in common.

Jesus was born in a stable at the back of an inn in Bethlehem, Palestine. Gautama was born under a tree in Lumbini, Nepal, while his mother, Queen Maya Devi, was traveling homewards to give birth. Jesus never knew his earthly father. A homeless teenager, named Mary, gave birth to Jesus. Gautama never knew his mother, who died a week after his birth.

Jesus spent his childhood with Mary and Joseph (his stepfather) in Nazareth, where Jesus learnt his stepfather's trade as a carpenter. Jesus probably never went to school while Gautama received the best education available. King Suddho*dana* and his aunt, Prajapati, gave Prince Gautama a life of luxury, including several servants to attend to all his needs. There is an enormous contrast in the upbringing of Jesus and Gautama.

Gautama lived a pampered life in palaces until he fled in his 30th year to seek out the Truth about life. There have been countless speculations about the so-called "missing years" of Jesus between the age of 12 and 30 years before he began giving teachings in Palestine.

In his three short years of teaching, Jesus spoke of the heart's liberation through love as his vision for humanity. Despite the military occupation and colonization of the Roman Empire, many in the Jewish community and others were desperate to listen to profound teachings from a man among them who spoke from his direct experience. No wonder such large crowds listened to the rabbi from Nazareth.

In Buddhist legends, written long before the gospels, the Buddha came down from heaven and entered into the womb of Queen Maya of the Sakyan people so she remained "undefiled." This legend has no relevance to Dharma teaching and practice but is an interesting parallel to the claims of the virgin birth of Jesus. As a boy, the wisdom of Jesus revealed itself in a meeting with the rabbis in Jerusalem. At around the same age, the compassion of Gautama revealed itself when he rescued a swan that his cousin, Devadatta, had shot through the neck with an arrow.

The *New Testament* and the Buddhist sutras have stories of Jesus and Gautama respectively at the age of 12. At the age of 12, Jesus disappeared in Jerusalem. His mother found him in the temple where he amazed the rabbis with his wisdom. Gautama recalled it when he was older about the same age sitting under a tree as a boy where he had a deep experience pointing the way to liberation.

Jesus and Gautama treated people equally and both remained totally committed to living a simple life based on love, kindness and acts of giving (*dana*). Non-violence, love, joy, Truth and freedom without attachment serve as common themes of the two teachers. Both point to liberation, not of the mundane world. Jesus called liberation the *Kingdom of Heaven* and Buddha referred to liberation as *Nirvana*. Both shared a great love of the Infinite and questioned the constructs of the finite. They offered teachings to dissolve the gap between the Infinite and the finite.

The time has come for Dharma practitioners and thoughtful people to resurrect Jesus from the Church and the Bible, and for Jesus to be a pillar of support, a transcendent voice reminding us of the importance of staying focused on love and a deathless realisation. If that is going to happen, it will require a dedicated exploration of the Dharma of Jesus. Practitioners need to be very clear about his statements on relative Truth and his inspired utterances on Ultimate Truth. Few religious authorities in human history remain unwavering in this regard. Jesus is one. Gautama is another. The focused voice of Jesus on love matters as much as ever. He has been an archetype for fearless love in our culture for 2000 years.

Jesus spoke with a depth that astounded the rabbis, Pharisees and scribes, as well as the poorest of the poor, the sick and the mad. He enthralled his followers with his stories, lucid explanations of his realizations of the Infinite (*Kingdom of Heaven*) and his powerful use of family metaphors, such as God the Father. Jesus knew his audience intimately, he knew that Middle Eastern culture treasured family life, and so he spoke to them in a language of family metaphors they appreciated such as God the Father as ultimate Truth and God the Son as relative Truth. We know Truth as that which transforms our life or the life of another. Truth releases into life and authentic love, compassion and wisdom. We cannot confine Truth to a few concepts, whether religious, scientific, spiritual or secular.

What Jesus and Buddha said

There are too many parallels between the Buddha and Jesus for us to ignore, too many similar statements about love, letting go, the path, the goal, inner change, ethics, concentration, wisdom, relative and Ultimate Truth. Did Jesus discover the great Truths of love and life through exposure to India in its era of dynamic inquiry into the self and beyond? To dive deeply into the Dharma teachings of Jesus, we must free ourselves from Christian orthodoxy.

Some Buddhists believe that Jesus could be considered a *bodhisattva*, a saintly man, an apocalyptic teacher, a founder of a religion, a religious radical or simply a wandering monk. These same Buddhists would hesitate to acknowledge his message as utterly in accord with the Dharma of the Buddha. It seems to me that these speculations are of no relevance as the original teachings themselves are profoundly spiritual and wise.

The Catholic Church replaced Jesus as the vehicle to find God and made the Church itself into the ultimate authority. The Protestant Church relegated Jesus and instead claimed The Bible - from the first page of Genesis to the last page of Revelations, as the word of God. Yet, leaders of both Catholics and Protestants have conspired to make Jesus the supreme religious figure of history and referred to him as

112

the only Son of God. Once the Church made Jesus the one and only Son of God, then believers could worship Jesus, sing his praises and go down on bended knee, without the need to explore and develop his teachings on the Way or realise the nature of the Kingdom of Heaven. Belief replaced realisation. The Church has subsequently persuaded the vast majority of Christians that accessing the Kingdom of Heaven occurs only after death. It is the absolute separation of Heaven from Earth and shows an alarming ignorance of the teachings of Jesus who advocated immediate access to the Kingdom of Heaven.

It is hardly surprising that many Westerners involved in Dharma practice were originally Christians through birth, education or belief. They become disillusioned with the Church's attitude. One can be a Christian and kill on behalf of the nation state, accumulate vast hordes of wealth regardless of the suffering of others, and pursue fame and power or secularist or Buddhist. Not surprisingly, many practicing Buddhists consciously steer away from Christianity, its dogma and its claims to being the "one true faith." The requirement to believe reveals the problem of any dogma.

The doctrines of the virgin birth and the physical resurrection of Jesus from the dead have no direct bearing whatsoever on what Jesus actually said. Church leaders and theologians uphold such bizarre beliefs as facts, as Truth, rather than mystical statements on purity (the Virgin birth) or our capacity to transcend death (the resurrection). The Church refers to these beliefs as physical facts and treats unresolved doubts in these core beliefs as a "crisis of faith."

A Welcome Relief

The down-to-earth teachings offered in the Buddha Dharma come as a welcome relief when compared to the dogma of Christianity. I recall one of my many meetings with Ajahn Dhammadharo of Thailand. I expressed doubt about the existence of the Buddha as a person. I expressed doubt about the belief in his claim of "complete, unexcelled enlightenment." I expressed doubts about Buddhism and the 227 rules (*Vinaya*) that all Buddhist monks in the Theravada tradition have to observe. I dismissed belief in rebirth and the heavenly realms as physical realities. The Christian equivalent would be to doubt God, doubt Jesus, and doubt the authority of the Church.

Ajahn Dhammadharo and the monks listening to my doubts simply shrugged their shoulders. "Mai pen rai" (never mind), he replied. "You don't have to believe in the Buddha, enlightenment, the rules or the religion. You do not even have to make mention of these matters. It does not matter whether you believe or not. See what works for you in your own experience. Keep practicing meditation."

I had not anticipated this answer. I expected to hear some concern. I thought my revered Dharma teacher would assume that I had become ensnared in a problematic state of mind, a hindrance to clarity. Far from it. He could not see the relevance of these beliefs in Buddha or Buddhism. He trusted in my meditation practice to find out what matters. It would be hard to imagine Christianity totally disregarding all reference to God, Jesus, the Bible or the Church. Christianity depends for the existence on its interpretation of these four words. Is it any wonder that conventional Christianity seems to have such little relevance for non-believers?

Palestine and India

When Jesus spoke in Palestine, he took enormous risks in giving uncompromising teachings of love and liberation. His resolute message cost him his life. He communicated with Jewish high priests, Roman soldiers, tax collectors, criminals and untouchables making the closest of friends and greatest of enemies. As a warning to others, the Roman authorities flogged, tortured and executed those who gained an independent following, including those with the most non-violent of philosophies.

Five hundred years before Jesus, the Buddha taught in India, the world's epicentre for spiritual inquiry, religious diversity and philosophical exploration. He addressed a well-educated and sophisticated culture that supported deep thinkers, renunciates, Brahmins, spiritual seekers, meditators, yogis, ascetics, mystics and profoundly realised human beings. The languages of India at the time, such as Pali, were dialects of Sanskrit, which has a strong emphasis on spiritual and psychological analysis. Every word had a precise and subtle meaning. Royal families, rulers and householders fully supported the spiritual nomads, encouraged their practices, treasured their wisdom and recognised their importance to society. A tolerant, spacious and intelligent society loved, trusted and respected their wise teachers.

The Roman Empire exercised tight and cruel control over the lives of those under the rule of Caesar. The contrast between Palestine and India in terms of the social/religious/political environment could hardly be greater. Palestine consisted of a largely illiterate, poverty stricken Jewish population of farmers and fishing villages, oppressed by occupation as well as religious dogmas in the hands of the high priests and Pharisees. Jesus refused to compromise. He spoke straightforwardly to the oppressed in such a misery-ridden corner of the world. Jesus inspired people to place the power of love in the forefront of priorities, no matter what.

Jesus revealed the transcendent reference point to this tormented and ugly world of brutal human behaviour. He shared the same voice of the Buddha, spoke of similar issues, and never wavered in staying true to love and liberation - even when Pontius Pilate, the Roman ruler over Palestine, ordered his soldiers to hammer a crown of thorns into his head, subjected him to lashings across his back and finally, naked and humiliated, had him nailed to the cross in front of his mother and Mary of Magdala.

Though the Buddha experienced occasional threats to his life, he taught the Dharma for 45 years from the age of 35 to 80 – a privilege denied to Jesus, who taught for three years.

The Meaning of the *Lord's Prayer*

The *Lord's Prayer* (Luke 11.2) is the most beloved of all prayers in Christendom containing short, poetic statements on ultimate and relative Truth.

The *Lord's Prayer* captures, in a succinct way, the heart of the teachings of Jesus. Not surprisingly, virtually everyone brought up in any Christian tradition, Catholic or Protestant, liberal or fundamentalist, knows by heart the *Lord's Prayer*. The prayer, a statement of the deepest Truths, has struck a chord in the hearts of Christians for 2000 years. Christians often overlook its most profound significance. Christians recite the prayer with mantra like repetition instead of a mindful and deliberate reflection. Jesus warned against unconscious recital of his prayer (the Aramaic word is *shela* which means to *'incline towards while abiding in a sublime inner space.'*) Jesus called upon us to lead a life of *prayer* in daily life, a meditative and mindful life always receptive to Truth. He gave the short prayer after the students of his teachings asked for instructions on how to pray.

Like the Buddha and other sages of India, Jesus offered open-air *satsang* (*sat* – Truth, *sang* – Sangha, gathering of the ones who love Truth). On a hill in Galilee, Jesus offered the Sangha the *Lord's Prayer*. The prayer consists of 52 words in the English translation.

> *"Our Father in heaven*
> *hallowed be your name,*
> *your kingdom come,*
> *your will be done,*
> *on earth as it is in heaven.*
> *Give us today our daily bread.*
> *Forgive us our trespasses,*
> *as we also forgive those who trespass against us.*
> *And lead us not into temptation*
> *but deliver us from evil."*

In Matthew 6.6, it is stated that Jesus taught people how to pray but in a way different from what they had known. He dismissed forms of public prayer if it was used to 'be seen by others.' He told his audience: *"Go into your room, pray to your Father who is unseen."* For Jesus, prayer is primarily the silent act, the contemplative state of being. In true prayer, there is nothing to ask for. *"Do not keep babbling on"*, said Jesus. Jesus clearly had little regard for long prayers, hymns, religious services, recitations and mantras. *"You won't be heard"* because of many words, he warns.

In other words, if our prayers fill up our minds with words, requests and supplications to God, then we block off

117

our heart to a transcendent receptivity. *"Your Father knows what you need before you ask him,"* Jesus said. In our aloneness, we can forget ourselves; we are not trying to impress others with our presence at a religious service. Our anonymity and our silence of being provide the open doorway for the deepest Truths to come to us. In other words, God 'speaks' to us in such an inner space. The *Lord's Prayer* is essentially a short and powerful meditative reflection into Ultimate Truth and the conventional world.

The poetic language of the words of Jesus emerge from his heart, full of love for people.

Our Father in heaven

The word for *Father* is *Abba* in Aramaic (the language the Nazarene rabbi spoke). It means *Foundation*. *Abba* is based on AB in early Aramaic – meaning where all movements end, to a completion. *Abba* is the basis for everything and completion of everything – in the same way that all waves rise and fall in the Ocean. Heaven – *shem-aya* – implies *'that without limits'*. It is the Limitless, the Infinite, the Immeasurable, the All (Allah), One in the Many (Elohim). The measurable (such as birth, life and death) rests in the Immeasurable, as the waves belong to the Ocean. The plight of humans is to grasp onto the measurable, onto the waves, and become blinded to the ocean that is the foundation for the waves.

hallowed be your name

Jesus reminded his students to make sure they never forget the Father of all things, namely the Ultimate Truth. His practical teachings and insight into daily life serve as a preparation to know a timeless and liberating Truth. Single-

118

pointed on the highest goal, we will realise the Sacred that is indestructible, without beginning, middle or end.

your kingdom come

He encouraged his students to focus their lives on realising the Kingdom of Heaven available in the immediacy, always close at hand, closer than our than our streams of thoughts. The conventional world consists of nation states. Jesus pointed to the borderless kingdom. The Kingdom that Jesus referred to becomes obscured through '"sin" – which originally meant *to turn our back on what really matters* and to settle for the mundane, the superficial including our identification with a nation state and earthly kingdoms, fixed and determined by the mind of divisive people.

your will be done

In this fourth line, Jesus introduced non-separation between the Kingdom of Heaven and daily life into his prayer as a statement of deepest intimacy with liberating Truth. It is the inseparability of Ultimate Truth and relative Truth, of the transcendent and the ordinary – an essential message of the Buddha as the only noble way of life. Jesus reminded everyone that our spirit matters. In the Four Gospels, there are more than 100 references to the spirit – *ruha* – the word also means *breath, air, wind*. Jesus also referred to the Kingdom of Heaven on more than 100 occasions in the Gospels. He told his audience about the importance of the breath as a vehicle to bridge the link between God and ourselves. Life breathes us in and breathes us out. *'Your will be done.'* The Buddha gave profound teachings on mindfulness of breathing (M118).

on earth as it is in heaven

Jesus warmed even more to his theme by ending the gap between heaven and earth. A life that has bridged heaven and earth reveals the deeper rhythms of life, contributes to revealing the emptiness of self and other, here and there, above and below, transcendent and conventional. This enables us to know the true nature of things, free from the tyranny and preoccupations of the narcissistic and isolated self.

give us today our daily bread

At the material level, people need the basic needs for food, clothing, shelter and medicine. Thoughtful people are grateful for access to these necessities on a daily basis. Starving people around the world do not have the privilege of the exploration into spiritual matters as their days remain focused on survival for themselves and their families. At a spiritual level, *bread* means that which nourishes us. An inner silence turns towards deep nourishment daily; we become available to ultimate insights and revelations. These uplift our spirit releasing joy and deep inner peace. This is the bread of life. This is the *Lord's Prayer* for all of us.

forgive us our trespasses

It is an extraordinary thing to participate in this adventure of life, to share with countless others the intimacy of dwelling on Earth. The Kingdom of Heaven is amongst us. When we acknowledge fully our transgressions, we liberate ourselves from the weight of the past. We know the true nature of forgiveness. We let go of our foolishness and unhealthy behaviour that trespass against the sacredness of

120

life. To forgive means to return to our true nature, free from selfishness, blame and guilt. We can learn to forgive ourselves, to forgive others and receive the forgiveness of others.

as we forgive those who trespass against us

Again, Jesus called upon us to dissolve the differences between each other. The dishing out of blame makes life miserable for all concerned. It is the basis for unwise action, sometimes leading to violence and war crimes. We inflict anguish and sorrow upon others when we ignore their feelings for our own selfish ends. And others trespass also upon us. Jesus reminded us of our capacity to see through these aberrations of human life; he encouraged us to love (that is respect) ourselves, love and respect others including those who trespass against us, abuse and harm us. Forgiveness also means freedom from any negativity and blame used to justify the inflicting of pain upon others. It is far more than an expression of a kindly understanding of their behaviour. Liberation from blame dissolves the gap between self and other enabling a meeting of heaven and earth.

and lead us not into temptation

Jesus and Buddha reminded us that even when established in the foundation of all things, temptations might still arise – as both Jesus and Buddha very occasionally experienced when encountering Satan or *Mara* (namely the forces of temptation). We may feel tempted to find ways to prove how great we are or how enlightened we have become. If we identify with temptations (the devil in us), we will suffer sooner or later. Even for the wise, temptations can arise through an inner movement leaning towards grasping onto the transitory and insubstantial. There are temptations to pursue power, status, position, sensuality as well as personal material gain regardless of its insubstantiality from a larger perspective. Challenges arise from within and without, but such forces do not have to lead us into conflict and struggle with forces within ourselves or within others. The most enlightened of human beings live with vigilance. Both the Buddha and Jesus saw how the mind can set a trap or offer bait. (Middle Length Discourse of the Buddha MLD 25).

and deliver us from evil

Evil not only includes the deliberate intent to inflict suffering upon others, but also refers to ignoring the opportunity to dissolve our projections, preoccupations and obsessions with the mundane. In Aramaic, *'good'* means to be *'ripe.'* It is an *'evil '* to be *'unripe'* for Truth. Truth and love transforms the inner life. Nothing else can. Truth blesses us when it touches the depth of our being to uncover indescribable realisations and natural joy. The *Lord's Prayer* points to the most profound of realisations. In the space of a few words, Jesus captured, with exquisite sensitivity, the very essence of all spiritual teachings. He expressed in a few short lines one of the greatest statements on Truth ever uttered on this Earth.

A selection of other statements of Truth stated by Jesus

The Buddhist reader of the gospels needs to be willing to make a significant shift in language, metaphors and analogies so that the Dharma of Jesus has an opportunity to make an impact. A cursory reading of the words of Jesus in the Gospels is not enough. His words on the way of transcendent understanding require meditation, reflection and a single pointed dedicated interest. The words of Jesus must speak directly to us, register in that 'place' even deeper than the heart to reveal the treasures of Truth. We should not confuse the Kingdom of Heaven in the teachings of Jesus and the temporary states of heavenly abiding referred to by the Buddha.

I admit the regular use of the family metaphor by Jesus of *Father* is not helpful for the West as it gives rise to the notion of a personal male God reinforcing a patriarchal society, though the family metaphor remains much in use in the Middle East and Mediterranean countries.

If you believe Jesus truly advocated a personal God, rather than employed metaphors, then it would be better to keep away from the Jesus and stay with the Buddha's teachings. I certainly prefer the direct language of the Buddha as that leaves no room for a personal God in any shape or form. If your mind can get over family metaphors and Christian doctrines, you may discover the same Truth that Jesus referred to with such poetic elegance and determination.

A Dharma View on some Profound Statements of Jesus

From the Four Gospels, I have selected major statements of Jesus on Truth with a very brief reflection as a small pointer to the potential for uncovering a treasure of love, insight and liberation. Meditations on the succinct words of Jesus have the capacity to open the heart to the Kingdom of Heaven.

Blessed are the poor in spirit, for yours is the Kingdom of Heaven.
Blessed are the meek: for they shall possess the land.
Blessed are they who mourn: for they shall be comforted.

Blessed are they that hunger and thirst after justice: for they shall have their fill.
Blessed are the merciful: for they shall obtain mercy.
Blessed are the clean of heart: for they shall see God.
Blessed are the peacemakers: for they shall be called children of God.
Blessed are they that suffer persecution for justice' sake, for theirs is the kingdom of heaven.
(Matthew 5.3)

In the discourse on the mountain, Jesus began with this much loved statement and ultimate expression of Truth. To realise that we are poor in spirit, rather than rich in spirit, means we have nothing whatsoever to possess as our own, as "I", "me" or "mine." The realisation of non-ego, non-possessiveness, non-clinging, non-craving around anything whatsoever reveals the Kingdom of Heaven. There is a liberating discovery through seeing the emptiness of the self and the poverty of the self.

The poor in spirit have given up the pressure of the rules, the precepts, the commandments, the religious laws and the identification with the beliefs. The poor in spirit have seen the emptiness of all the forms, religious services and methodology. The Kingdom of Heaven liberates all from the burden of religious legalisms, theology, and the effort to support and defend beliefs.

Here Jesus shares the same voice as the Buddha, who said that as the precepts, rules and vows increase, then the number of fully liberated ones decreases.

"The Kingdom of Heaven is like a mustard seed that a man took and planted in his field. Though it is the smallest of all your seeds, yet when it grows, it is the largest of garden plants and

becomes a tree so that the birds of the air come and perch in its branches." (Matthew 13.31)

Jesus told of the mustard seed that grows to become a shrub and then a tree, giving shelter to the birds. There are no boundaries to the Kingdom of Heaven. Heaven is infinite and with infinite potential. Jesus makes this point in this simile. The Kingdom of Heaven is both large and small. The Kingdom of Heaven communicates in the tiniest expression of life, yet that tiny expression carries extraordinary potential. The story of the mustard seed is given three times in the Gospels struck a chord with Matthew, Mark and Luke, who referred to the analogy in their accounts of the life of Jesus.

There is a deliberate twist in the analogy that Jesus offers. There are only mustard plants. There is no such thing as a mustard tree. We see beautiful fields of yellow mustard plants in Palestine and elsewhere, a delight to witness. If left to grow from these tiny seeds, these plants may reach three or four metres in height. What is Jesus saying? He is not concerned with cause and effect since the mustard seed cannot become a tree. In the finite, even in the smallest particle, there is the expression of the infinite. There is the revelation of something very small, including a sub atomic particle, to show its infinite potential to reveal far more than what it is. Love and attention to the detail, the particular, makes infinite revelations possible.

In this beautiful analogy, Jesus reminded his listeners that the Kingdom of Heaven is immediately accessible, revealing itself as much in the tiniest seed as in the vastness of cosmic life. Jesus loved the earth, the desert; he wandered in the fields and forests of Palestine, where he had worked as a carpenter. He realised that the Infinite reveals itself in the very small and finite as much as in the sense of the vast

125

and universal. Love and liberation dissolves the entrapment in the false world of egotism. It would be worthwhile to take a single mustard seed, place it in the hand, and meditate on it until the Truth of its infinitude emerges.

"Your Father in heaven makes the sun rise on the evil and on the good, and sends rain on the righteous and on the unrighteous." (Matthew 5:45)

There would be little point in taking these words about the weather as literal statements since what would be the point in stating the blindingly obvious. In this statement, Jesus turned from the relative Truth of path, practice and goal to the immediacy of realisation to the Truth, just as he did in the *Lord's Prayer.* Jesus spoke from a liberated perspective. He boldly stated that Truth pervades the wholesome and the unwholesome The human constructs of hierarchy in the sentient realm, good over bad, bad over good, right over wrong or wrong over right, and the litany of differences that seem to perpetuate themselves through daily life, have much less significance through realising that the sun shines and the rain falls equally over all.

"Foxes have holes, and the birds of the air have nests but the son of man has nowhere to lay his head." (Luke 9:58)

The conventional interpretation indicates the homeless way of life of Jesus, but the son of man (that family metaphor again, not a messianic designation) refers to our true nature - free from a location, a place, a time, nor seeking shelter in any kind of form. There is nothing for our mind to lean on.

"You shall know the Truth that sets you free." (John 8.32). Jesus gave a teaching on homelessness in the conventional sense

126

but more importantly, he spoke from the deepest sense. In accordance with the true nature of things, there is no home, no fixed abode in the everyday realm. Freedom shows itself when not tied down.

"It is easier for a camel to go through the eye of a needle than for a rich man to enter the Kingdom of God." (Matthew 9.23)

Jesus reiterated his words again with another powerful statement about realisation. How hard it is for those who have wealth to enter the Kingdom of God – harder than for a camel to go through the eye of a needle. When men and women walked out of the householders' life and the duties and social responsibilities that accompanied such a role, they asked the Buddha: "What should we call ourselves?" The Buddha replied *"bhikkhu"* and *"bhikkhunis"* – words meaning *male* and *female beggars.* In other words, having no special status, no clinging to a career, no particular role. Having seen the emptiness of self-existence and anything belonging to a self, the eye of the needle is wide open.

"Do not store up for yourselves treasures on earth, where moth and rust destroy. Store up for yourselves treasures in heaven." (Matthew 6.19)

Jesus made the difference clear between conventional standpoints and ultimate priority. What does it matter to accumulate wealth when everything acquired eventually gets eaten up or rusts away? If our wealth does not disappear due to misadventure, then nature will gradually erode a person's life until it is finished. It is an important reminder that all acquisitions are transitory and not worth making into objects of clinging. Truth is full of ageless treasures.

"Give to Caesar what is Caesar's and to God what is God's." (Matthew 22.21)

When Jesus spoke these words, his listeners might have concluded that Jesus was telling his audience to pay their taxes to the Roman Empire. Perhaps he wanted to show that he spoke as a dutiful citizen to please the Roman occupiers of Palestine, but it seems unlikely. Jesus looked at a coin handed to him before uttering these words. He had no regard for political conventions, power, money or personal approval. The gospel says that his listeners did not know how to interpret what Jesus said. He stated that the Kingdom of Heaven is not a compromise between worldly conventions and ultimate realisation. What goes to Caesar is small change. *Abba*, the foundation of everything, takes priority.

"You are the salt of the Earth, but if the salt loses its saltiness, how can you be made salty again?" (Matthew 5.13)

Jesus speaks of the significance of being fully human, fully conscious, knowing a profound sense of love. This statement reminds me of the Buddhist teachings of the blessings of human birth. Due to consciousness, there is the potential for full awakening to the power of love. If we live unconscious lives, we have a bland existence – like food without salt – showing little love.

"First take the plank out of your own eye, and then you will see clearly to remove the speck from your brother's eye." (Matthew 7.5)

Jesus consistently reminded us to work on ourselves, to dissolve the distortions in the way we see. Seeing clearly reveals the Ultimate Truth. It dissolves the dirt in the eye of perceiver.

"The one who received the seed that fell on good soil is the man who hears the word and understands it. He produces a crop yielding a hundred, sixty or thirty times what was sown." (Matthew 13.23)

If we understand the teachings, then seeds of Truth enter deep into our being bringing about benefits far beyond the initial experience and immediate insights. We know the power of living with love as our first priority from one day to the next.

"The Kingdom of Heaven is like a treasure hidden in a field. When a man found it, he hid it again, and then in his joy went out and sold all that he had and bought that field." (Matthew 13.44)

Profound realization and transformative experience opens the door to countless insights, joy, deep love and endless treasures of liberating Truth. Far too many live in the field of mundane existence fascinated and spellbound by what comes to the senses. Through digging deep into the field, treasures suddenly become available beyond anything available to our senses. Everything else seems of minor consideration. The wise happily give up all possessiveness, all attachments, to go deep into the limitless field of countless treasures.

"Every teacher of the Law who has been instructed about the Kingdom of Heaven is like the owner of a house who brings out of his storeroom new treasures as well as old." (Matthew 13.52)

Truth is infinite in its expression. There is the capacity to realise fresh perspectives on Truth and share with others. We protect Truth when we acknowledge our views express a perspective rather than an absolute position.

"With God all things are possible." (Matthew 19.26)

If we concentrate on *Abba*, the birthless foundation of what matters, then Truth makes everything possible. There are no limits to discovery, to revelations and the immensity of our heart and mind.

"The Kingdom of God is near." (Mark 1.14)

This is usually taken to mean *"it is coming soon."* Commentators have tended to interpret this as 'only a matter of time.' Jesus means something quite different. The Kingdom of God is closer than all of our thoughts.

"Watch out for the yeast of Pharisees and of Herod." (Mark 8.14)
Be mindful of the claims of religious and ruling authorities.

"No one can see the Kingdom of God unless he is born again." (John 3.3)

The transformation of a human being is greater than the transformation of a grub in a cocoon into a butterfly.

"You will look for me but you will not find me." (John 7.34)

This is the language of the Kingdom of Heaven. Jesus did not identify himself with body/mind and so remained untraceable and unfixable.

"My Kingdom is not of this world." (John 18.36)

The ordinary world does not define the Kingdom. It is not of this world, yet to imagine that it is somewhere else makes for a false dichotomy. He said *"heaven and earth must pass away"* to dissolve the gap, the separation. Liberation knows that the self and other as apart from each other belongs to mental constructions rather than true reality.

Jesus and access to the Kingdom of Heaven

Access to the Kingdom of Heaven requires a single pointed and unwavering dedication; otherwise, Jesus warned, we would be like a slave who serves two masters, namely the mundane world and Truth. We will find ourselves in conflict, loving one, hating the other, devoted to one and fighting the other. We will become trapped in different priorities. Dedication requires sacrifice of the mundane, namely desires, demands and clinging. Nobody can realise liberating Truth without sacrifice. Jesus and Buddha never tire of reminding us of this.. We cannot serve Truth and hang onto self-interest, even when couched in the language of needs and desire for security. Jesus said, *"No one who puts his hand to the plough and looks back is fit for the Kingdom of God."*(Luke 9.62).

If we look back, we easily dwell in the past, make all manner of claims about our achievements or feel to be a prisoner to our history. We put our hand to the plough. We turn the soil over. We see afresh. We wake up to Truth.

Three commonly held views of liberation

There are three commonly held views of liberation, of the Kingdom:

1. *It is a once in a lifetime experience.*
2. *We can go in and out of liberation.*
3. *We believe that liberation, itself, is impermanent; that it comes and goes like everything else.*

All three viewpoints depend on one's interpretation. Some Buddhists grasp onto the interpretation of their personal experience or their interpretation of the Buddha's night of his full awakening. The realization of the realm of liberation exposes its potential to reveal more than what is apparent. Is it any wonder that Jesus told his listeners that, once having discovered the treasure then to go back to the field of endless treasures?

It seems highly unlikely that the Buddha, with his commitment to serving the Dharma for 45 years, based his teachings narrowly on a single experience under the tree. That experience would have become a distant memory in the passage of time. He continued to discover numerous further treasures of insights over the years in this 'field' that has no signs, no characteristics, no coming, nor going, nor entering, nor losing touch with.

Orthodox religious leaders could not comprehend Jesus when he spoke of such things. What he pointed to seemed so far away from their theological beliefs and religious laws.

The religious authorities, with their rites and rituals, demanded that Jesus give a clear sign of the immediacy of the Kingdom of God. Jesus responded identically to the Buddha when he said, *"Why does this generation ask for a sign.*

Truly, I tell you, no sign will be given." (Mark 8.11-12) Similarly, the Buddha said liberation is signless.

"To you have been given the secret of the Kingdom of God but for those outside everything comes in parables." (Mark 4.11 and 34)

The Buddha also uncovered the secret for profound liberation so we can know awakening with its infinite treasures, which remain hidden in this world.

Liberation expresses a freedom from the weights of the past, a freedom to be in the present with inner peace and wisdom and the freedom to act with love and compassion.

All three kinds of freedom reflect a fully integrated liberation intimate with knowing causation and contingency factors without dependency.

Let us sit up and take a deep interest in the teachings of Jesus. Let us regard Jesus as our *kalyana mitta.*

Chapter 8

The Longing for Intimacy

*One makes an end to suffering by abandoning the underlying
tendency to the lust for pleasant feelings. MN 148.34*

It is unfortunate that the Buddha had no experience of
intimate love with a woman after his realisations under the
Bodhi Tree. If he did, he would surely have devised the Noble
Ninefold Path to include Right Relationship, rather than the
Noble Eightfold Path. He seems to have taken the view that a
human being depends upon desire, an unsatisfactory force, to
make love. It is understandable since he advocated a celibate
and nomadic way of life. The Buddha seems to have accepted
the traditional Indian viewpoint that celibacy had a greater
value on the path of awakening than making love. His view
has had long-term consequences. In light of present
experiences and understanding, it is time to fully include
relationships and intimacy as equally supportive for full
awakening as celibacy; generally speaking, the ordained
Sangha of Buddhism continues to resist this viewpoint.

The Buddha tended to extol the virtues of the homeless
wandering seeker rather than family life or for couples or
singles. He described a householders' life as *"crowded and
dusty"* while *"a life gone forth is wide open."* (MN36). That
generalisation may have rung true in caste-ridden,
housebound India 2600 years ago, but for many of us today
our homes are neither crowded nor dusty (unlike some
monasteries!), and we have the freedom to explore wide-open
spaces as well. The situation has reached the ironic position
today where monasteries are often crowded while monks and
nuns have to spend much time keeping them free from dirt

134

and dust. Meanwhile householders, individuals and families, can wander the world for weeks, months or years, living a nomadic life carrying only a backpack.

In the days before contraception, relationships almost inevitably led to children and subsequent commitments. The lack of contraception influenced religious views about sex and celibacy. Today condoms, the cap, the pill or a vasectomy, generally enable a reliable separation of sex from procreation. This is a modern and welcome development. To be fair, the Buddha could not have predicted such radical changes in society. Some religious leaders claim that sex is purely for pro-creation while secular culture often uses sex for the pleasure of securing intense sensations, selling products or promoting the self. The act of making love has the potential to reveal deep spiritual sensitivities and a profoundly erotic sharing.

Yet the Buddha did not adopt a prudish outlook towards the body. For example, he displayed a liberal attitude around nakedness. For years, the homeless followers of the Dharma, both men and women, bathed naked together in the rivers, streams and beneath the waterfalls in the Sakyan and neighbouring kingdoms of northern India. He showed a remarkable confidence in his networks of practitioners to appreciate the human form without abusing trust in each other.

The Buddha's support for public nakedness at bathing times surely helped dissolve sexual obsessions through *seeing body as body* – to use an important insight of the Buddha. The nomadic Sangha, both men and women, wore only a piece of cloth wrapped around the waist and another piece of loose cloth to keep the sun off the upper part of the body. Even in our so-called more enlightened times, Buddhist meditators of both sexes never shower naked together on retreats. The Buddha's relaxed approach to nakedness, for himself and others, must have shocked the conservative Brahminical tradition of ancient India when they heard about the naked bathing of his followers. This liberal attitude would also have offended the yogis, nearly all men, who led lives of solitude while struggling to overcome their desires of the flesh through intensive self-punishing practices.

It was unfortunate that after years of teaching, the Buddha agreed to a request by Visakha, a lay woman, to provide a cloth for his free spirited wanderers to cover themselves whist bathing. Visakkha told the Buddha she could not distinguish naked men and woman who followed the Buddha from naked ascetics, or courtesans (high-class prostitutes) in the palaces who often bathed naked with their clients. The courtesans who were bathing in the same place as the Sangha, would tell the younger women practitioners to abandon celibacy and become celibate much later in life so that they could have the best of both worlds, i.e. worldly pleasure when young and religious happiness later in life when men were no longer interested in their sexual favours.

Until the era of British colonised India, the women of India wore the sari without any undergarments. Christian missionaries, in the Victorian era, persuaded Indian women to wear blouses and petticoats to cover themselves up. There are no words in Hindi for these garments and so the English words are still used.

Some Buddhist meditation traditions separate men from women in the meditation hall, fearful that meditators will experience feelings of attraction and sexual energy if men and women choose to sit where they wish in the hall. Some Buddhist traditions have separate gender communities as a way to minimise the arising of sexual energy in residential life. Looking positively, this may also enable people of the same gender to develop a depth of friendship. Such friendships may rarely happen in a society where people put their partner above all other relationships. Same gender communities can

136

also lead to heightened tension when the sexes do get together. The separation of the sexes in spiritual/religious practices tell us more about today's spiritual/religious leaders than anything else.

Times have changed. There is a more tolerant attitude among a number of Sanghas and spiritual circles in the West where nakedness is accepted rather than rejected. To take a small example, every summer in France, I lead an annual 10-day pilgrimage (*Yatra*) with the regular opportunity to camp besides a river or lake. Men, women and children can bathe naked, if they wish, in cooling water.

The Pali discourses (*suttas*) that contain the full body of the Buddha's teachings, throw only a few breadcrumbs of reflection towards matters of sex. The suttas offer a moral code around sexual behaviour: no sexual violence, abuse, manipulation, adultery, sex with minors or sex which can cause any kind of harm. The teachings extol virtue and sensitivity in matters of intimacy, but sadly ignore the value of love joined to a creative, erotic contact with another. Buddhism has limited teachings on sexuality aside from the application of moral guidelines. Outside of Tantra, there is barely any reference to love and sexuality belonging to Dharma practice of awakening. Furthermore, it is not easy to find Tantric texts that truly speak to dedicated Dharma practitioners.

To his credit though, the Buddha strongly endorsed first-hand experience in all matters over and above his views. The Buddha stressed the importance of finding wisdom through our own experiences rather than submissively taking on board the Buddha's standpoint. Dharma practice today for householders can include the exploration of love and sexual intimacy as one of many possible expressions to allow one to go deeper within and deeper into external situations. The wealth of inner life, devotion, love, energy and intimacy, become assesible to both partners in an atmosphere of mutual trust and respect. Many Buddhist monks and nuns, East and West, have listened to their inner longing for intimacy. They disrobed. They developed a relationship. They have no regrets.

Longing and Love

In the silence of meditation, in addition to the arising of fluctuating feelings and thoughts and images from daily life, the frustrated and unhappy meditator can easily cling to ideas of romantic love, including fantasies, projections and desires for the perfect partner. These yearnings arise from personal dissatisfaction and disappointment. Unhappiness around relationships – partners, friends and family – can effectively kill off the romance of life.

Those who long for romantic love will tend to be on the constant look out for a partner. These unresolved desires for romance and sexual intimacy often prove to be a 'turn-off" to another person. A depth of inner contentment allows romantic love to flow without yearning for it. It is valuable to distinguish clearly the full potential of romantic love and the harboured, unfulfilled wanting for intimacy. There is a world of difference between the two. If we are happy and undemanding, we will experience precious communications with another that may lead to the development of a committed relationship. Otherwise, others will sense our unfulfilled desires within us and remain cautious.

An old rock 'n' roll song reminds us that we can't always get what we want. Unrequited attraction challenges our clarity around love and sex. It requires a total acknowledgement of the authenticity of our passion, even if the other person has little or no conception of the intensity of our interest towards him or her. It is not always easy to distinguish within ourselves the difference between an intense attraction and genuine love. Attraction towards or love for another or both attraction and love together may not be reciprocated. It is a matter of learning to abide in the depth of love, keep to a noble silence, and not imagine that circumstances would ever change.

Love and passion can fuse together. Such passion can stand on its own when benefitting from an undemanding recognition that it would be inappropriate to try to pursue the attention of the recipient. If there is anguish and pain, then desire, projections and fantasies distort the love. The Buddha pointed out that true love confirms what is divine but added that equanimity also expresses divinity. Equanimity provides a steadfast support to love when there is no reciprocation to our love. To witness beauty is to know love. Love recognises beauty and the witness of beauty experiences a divine realm of appreciative joy.

In the early 1990's, I recall spending a heavenly day with a woman of great Mediterranean beauty, inwardly and outwardly. On one of those sublime summer days on the Cornish coast, an area in the world that she loved to visit, we ambled together along the sandy beach through the late afternoon. At one point, I separated from her and was leaning against the edge of a cliff among the rocks, as she stood at the water's edge facing out to sea. Her natural beauty fused with all the beauty that surrounded her. It was a privilege to witness her in that moment with her calm and cool presence, and yet not know what was to happen between us. Wondrous times, such as this, consist of much more than the sum total of their parts, much more than two people walking in the afternoon. These occasions speak to us of the ineffable, the unmanufactured, of a boundless, limitless heart.

SHE STANDS IN BEAUTY

I recall aroma of lazy days,
your naked toes to touch as the sea plays,
at water's edge, a sole beauty I saw,
welcome the red evening sun and more.

Arched your long neck, dignity, beam of light,
sublime creature, you stand in calm twilight,
a sweetness beckons your true state to reach;
I felt my heart pulsing across the beach.

I felt your happiness, blue ocean near,
as you enjoyed the white-top waves so dear,
the spread of joy, a time to satisfy,
eternal waters as breath meets the sky.

I still recall you met with sun and sea,
silent to witness, you set yourself free;
I leaned back in rocks, remained still and sure,
a hanging back. Your cool embers held in store.

Poems from the Edge of Time.

Sometimes, it takes years of patience for love to find its expression with another, if at all and quiet longing can accompany love. At the age of 18 years, my Auntie Daisy worked at a market stall in a northern city in England selling chocolate. George, 32, a married man, worked in the next stall selling fruit and vegetables. She told me she fell in love with him and she kept this a secret. More than 30 years later, George's wife died. A few years after, Daisy and George married and shared 16 years of happiness with each other. It is an account of romantic love tempered, year after year, with patience. Of course, not all such stories of patience, with years of unrequited love, have a happy conclusion. Love can offer no guarantees. It takes wisdom and love to deal with unwelcome, separations and death, as well as being patient with the sadness felt deep down in the being. It too will change and gradually fade through non-clinging.

Opening of Consciousness

There is at times a gap in communication between partners. One partner wants the other to share his or her experiences but there is only a deafening silence: the partner has an inability to listen. This situation in a relationship can become very painful. A partner can hold a secret from the other. The secrecy can destroy the relationship more than the content of the secret.

The poem below tells of a woman's decision to tell her partner that she had slept with another man and that the subsequent affair had been going on for some months, although it was now over. He had taken the confession from her very badly. She could see that his heart had gone cold as tears emerged from his eyes. She waited for him to respond, knowing that she should have spoken to him immediately after she became attracted to this other man. Her chance for forgiveness had gone, even though she tried to explain that the delay was caused by fears around telling him. She knew the cost of what had happened and knew the time had gone to heal their relationship.

A MAN BETRAYED

His heart had grown cold, a man betrayed,
his features cast away, a distant wall,
his lonely heart and slump that he displayed

just his eyes only left his tears to fall.

She had to wait again to hear his words
 and melt the ice that hid away his needs
she knew he lingers long, the time disturbs,
her chance had gone - despite what she then pleads.

All hope no more and all thoughts had rotted,
she knew the meaning of word and deed,
she knew the cost of what she had plotted,
her time had gone to meet his soul and need.

Poems from the Edge the Edge of Time

A relationship is a reflective practice on a daily basis. If it is not, the relationship may crumble owing to the weight of what the couple have chosen to ignore. One partner may show awareness of blind spots while the other takes the relationship for granted. In time, the blind spots have an explosive impact on the relationship. The conscious partner notices the tell-tale signs of a problem, of tension in the air, of the unspoken that hangs heavily. Whereas, a seasoned love, a good friendship and ability to share on many levels, keeps a relationship strong, offering a certain relative security between two people with an understanding of each other's latent tendencies. In the dissolution of the passion to share and inquire, the couple will settle into a routine that lacks vitality. Their relationship will probably lack a creative love life with deep enjoyment of everyday adventures.

During many hours spent on Indian trains, passengers have asked me: "Are you one person or two?" – meaning are you a single man or do you have a wife? In a relationship, a person is neither one nor two. If both absorb into each other, they will lose the sense of themselves. If the partners do not absorb into each other, they will feel separation. The act of intimacy includes the sharing yet, at times, both partners need to experience their autonomy as an individual. If the two people become immersed in their own worlds, each will forget the qualities he or she feels for the other. If the two people do not experience any depth of immersion into each other, they will feel separation. Love is not about two people living as one person, or two persons living in their own worlds, nor is love about moving backwards and forwards between being as one with another, and being independent.

In times of personal turmoil, the inner life becomes vulnerable to the idealising of romantic love or becoming cynical about it. With the former view, a person imagines a fairy-tale love affair: a handsome Prince sweeps us off our feet, a beautiful Princess wants to share her life with us. Or a person lives in the dream of a Hollywood movie with its happy-ever-after ending. One woman in Israel told me "I cannot find in the world, the man to match the man of my dreams within me." That man does not exist, that's why!

Some have to endure a relationship with a partner who becomes increasingly more possessive. One woman told me that her partner wanted the two of them to be together every moment of the day. At first, she felt swept along with such a commitment. They did everything together from wake up to sleep, never apart. She felt he was totally committed to her and her to him. However, after a couple of years, she began to feel restricted living in a state of merging her whole being with her partner, even though she had fantasised about such love for years. "I couldn't breathe" she said. Her concerns about the intensity of their relationship began to grow. He did not like her going out without him to see her friends, or even reading a book alone at home. When she protested, he became aggressive – followed by sincere apologies for his abusive language. Then once he hit her for going out in the evening without him. Terrified, she fled from home and moved overseas to stop him from finding her.

Relationships can go through phases of disillusionment where the partner is seen as painfully separate. Romantic love requires the support of calm presence, an undemanding attitude, deep friendship and the capacity to accommodate changes. 'Oneness' is not a higher state than 'Twoness' – nor the other way around. No state is worth clinging to. Being with another and being with oneself matter equally.

In the Connected Discourses (SN 1 173-174) the Buddha offered wise counsel on relationships:

> *"People cannot be known well by their appearance,*
> *Nor can they be trusted after a brief impression,*
> *Yet the undisciplined may roam in the world*
> *In the attire of the well-disciplined.*
>
> *Some adorn their unpleasantness*
> *With pretended suave action*
> *Like a clear ear ring or brass*
> *Painted with glittering gold."*

These two verses close with a powerful metaphor. Using his memory and power of observation, the Buddha said that a man and woman can become bound initially to each other in eight ways:

- *form*
- *smiles*
- *words*
- *singing*
- *crying,*
- *manner*

- *a gift*
- *touch.*

He warned men against becoming a "woman hunter" (*itthidbutto*). He said engaging in numerous sexual relationships "drains" the inner life making one feel empty. There is a constant encouragement to express gentle speech and never use harsh words. This expresses an awareness of the sensitivities of both women and men. And, in the third verse of the Dhammapada, the Buddha warned against clinging to any past misdeeds of another.

A wish to develop a relationship can go towards

- *an authority figure*
- *family*
- *a group*
- *a lifestyle*
- *a place*
- *a vision*
- *a wish to develop a relationship can also go towards:*
- *an activity*
- *a person where it is not possible to form a relationship because of the distress it would cause*
- *a person who is not sure whether he or she wishes to start a relationship*
- *a person with whom it is possible to form a relationship without causing another distress*

It is important to consider the different types of relationships that may matter to us, otherwise we can grasp after one and neglect the opportunity to develop other kinds or relationships.

Whether long or short in duration, the intimate relationship acts as a resource for knowing the divine nature of love and the activities of body, speech and mind confirming such love. There is no special virtue in either a long or short relationship; the virtue rests in the mutual exploration to deal with a variety of expressions of a relationship. The long history of making a spiritual virtue out of celibacy has left the impression in the minds of many Buddhists that total liberation and intimate relationship are incompatible. The Western Dharma tradition has the task of showing that this view is a myth, a smokescreen, a mirage, a notion that long since has gone past its 'sell by' date.

Marriage

It is the quality of the relationship in a marriage or committed partnership that matters, not quantity: not the length of time. There appear to be five primary reasons why two people stay together in a marriage, and the same relationship can know all five:

1. *Duty: The couple may have children who become the binding force to keep the couple together, or they remain together for social and economic reasons.*

2. *Religious obligation: The partners have taken religious vows 'until death do us part' and may as a couple simply not believe in divorce.*

3. *Force of habit: There is no motivation to make real changes. The alternative is separation, isolation and possibly loneliness. The thought of dividing property, bringing in the lawyers and explanation to friends and family inhibits steps to start a new life.*

4. *Love: The couple share their love, trust and friendship.*

5. *A path or expression of Awakening: The partnership or marriage is viewed as a real opportunity for the exploration and sharing of the light and dark areas within.*

There is an obligation towards children that needs immense consideration. With the first three reasons, the marriage may have developed into a very pale shadow of the original love that sparked that relationship. The couple have little left to say to each other except for the practicalities of daily life. Passion, adventure, making love becomes a very occasional event, if at all. There is little passion or no adventure, no sharing of the feelings and thoughts about each other, nor do the couple engage in creative use of their imagination to launch fresh projects. The two people assume they know each other but they probably know only each other's habits.

For other marriages or partnerships, love and friendship permeate the daily experience. The two people get on extraordinarily well together. There is a depth of contact and contentment in the relationship, whether or not the two people share much or little with each other about their inner lives. The two people may not even comprehend what a path of awakening means as that language is not their forte. Warmth, appreciation and loving presence pervade the marriage.

In the fifth kind of marriage, the two people are equally committed to making their relationship a path or expression of awakening. This requires a sharing of their deepest experiences, both joyful and painful. It includes a dialogue about their relationship with each other and about life itself. Ethics, values, meditations, reflections, issues from the personal to the global contribute to the path or expression of awakening. Both partners recognise and appreciate what they offer to each other. The fifth kind of partnership does not also offer a guarantee of long term security. Perhaps one partner or both cannot make such a commitment for the long term. The quality of relationship and the commitment to the heart's inquiry provide the raw material for insights and understanding for both partners for the duration of the relationship. Depth of communication matters in such a relationship, not the number of years spent together.

The Triangle

The Buddha referred to three things conducted in secrecy: a man and woman having an affair, mantras of the Brahmins and holding to wrong views. While three things shine openly: the moon, the sun and the Dharma (AN 111.129).

According to sociologists, marriages and long-standing partnerships often have to weather one partner feeling a very strong attraction towards somebody else, falling in love with another or starting an affair. Many couples work with such challenges to their marriage or partnership. Sometimes a long standing relationship may end, not because one or both are living in a wretched situation but due to the arising of forces of love for a third party.

Dedicated to his marriage and the Dharma for 25 years, a man told me he had fully expected to spend the rest of his life with his wife. They had a quiet, conventional, middle class life in the suburbs of the city where he worked. He then met a woman about 10 years younger than himself. They fell totally in love with each other and found every possible way to spend secretly as much time together as possible. He then told his wife. She told him that he had to make up his mind whether to stay in the marriage or leave it for the other woman.

He told me: "I could not believe that this was happening to me. I felt I was breaking the precept around sexual misconduct. Why would I want to jeopardise a secure marriage. I have never felt so challenged in all my life. I love two women for two different reasons. Both women say they love me. My power of love takes no notice of conventions, of orthodoxy. Falling in love has humbled me, shaken up all my views about myself, forced me to enter into deep communications with my wife and made me realise how little real control I have over my life." Love coupled with magnetic attraction often acts in more powerful ways than the voice of reason. Family and friends often fail to understand this when an important person in their life finds themselves in a 'ménage a trois.'

If we have the tendency to romanticise a person, pleasurable projections may not last long. It is vital to know the difference between the power of romantic love and romanticising an individual. The depth of chemistry between two people, or one for another, can generate all manner of sensations of excitement and anticipation in the pit of the stomach. Is it idealisation like a teenager meeting a big rock star? Or is it the powerful force of love and sexual energy fused and focussed on another? Love moves in more powerful ways than via bodily intimations. Authentic falling in love stands outside the superficiality of projections, breaks free from the past and engages in an intimate communication with another.

Morality

A Buddhist commentary referred to 'prescribed morality' as a set of fixed rules, precepts or guidelines (*pannatti-sila*) such as "I vow to be faithful to my partner."

Non-prescribed morality (*pakati sila*) emerges out of awareness, exploration and virtue and is not tied to rules. Dharma teachings question the prescribed morality of religion and society but appreciate the natural, non-prescribed morality born of practice, observation and experience knowing that no one can prescribe what is best for another. There is real virtue in non-prescribed morality because it emerges out of first-hand experience rather than conformity to rules and precepts.

True ethics makes wisdom and empathy with others shine. Wisdom makes ethics shine. When men and women find themselves facing passion for another outside of their marriage or relationship, their morality may appear very different from religious and social standpoints on the issue. The lover faces the depth of feelings for two people and their responses. Ethics include listening to the inner voice of the heart, even though it is outside of the prescribed morality.

A married woman who was attending one of my retreats recently, told me she had fallen in love with a handsome and caring man dedicated to the Dharma and meditation. She said she had reached the point where she could not handle the inner conflict any longer and so told her husband of her love affair with the younger man. In this *ménage a trois*, her close friends opted for prescribed morality. It did not help her to come to a wise response to her situation.

- *"You have two children. Don't be so selfish."*
- *"Why do you put yourself first?"*

- *"You have to let go of your lover."*
- *"It's just a fling."*
- *"You are using the lover to fill a hole in your life."*
- *"Your partner loves you. How can you betray his trust?"*

The woman also experienced these moralising voices within herself as self-blame and self-criticism. Although it was a relief to reveal her love affair to her husband, it did not resolve the issue even though he made it clear he had boundaries for their marriage. She felt enormous pressure to come to a decision. Identification with the prescribed morality inhibited the exploration of a less conventional and perhaps deeper morality: namely of being true to one's experience, true to love and true to the challenge of handling such circumstances wisely and expansively. This deeper morality ignores the conventions and the 'straightjacket' interpretation of a prescribed morality. In the deepest ethics, we have to remain true to something that is not easily resolvable in the *ménage a trois*. Not surprisingly, the issues of unresolved love can last for weeks, months or years. This does not indicate that those involved have become caught up in clinging but can demonstrate the capacity for patience and quiet endurance.

Each person in the *ménage a trois* must learn to take responsibility for their feelings, views and actions. It is too easy to blame another: E.g. "You are causing me so much suffering." Nobody in such a triangle finds it easy to take the heat in the situation or deal with the intensity of feelings around staying or leaving. Dharma practice includes taking responsibility for staying with the dynamics of such an event or withdrawing from it, and getting on with one's life in another way.

It is common that an affair, whether secret or not, can give the partner a sense of personal independence. The

151

triangle may appear at first glance to threaten a marriage but the impact of it may save a marriage or sustain it, to the surprise of all. We need to be mindful of casting judgements in the dynamics of intimate relationships unless we have a fully comprehensive picture from all the people involved. To understand the Dharma and the drama of a triangle, we need to understand the conditions of dependently arising circumstances in the lives of those involved.

I told the married woman that the power rests in her hands. I made it clear to her that this privilege stays for a period. It could move out of her hands and into the hands of her husband, her lover or other events. I said she should not force herself into a decision just because everybody keeps telling her it is the right thing to do. There is no point in betraying her heart. She has to be patient as long as necessary, to trust in an unconventional morality:

- *to be mindful,*
- *to reflect,*
- *to listen deeply inwardly,*
- *to see what emerges free from conventional pressure.*

She thanked me, and e-mailed me months later to say that the unresolved issue continued. A year or two later, she made the decision to live alone. "I am finally at peace with myself," she wrote. I hear such stories frequently enough. I know Dharma couples who have been engaged in a *ménage a trois* for several years, one partner or both have learnt skilfully to handle such unusual arrangements. For some it is open and discussed and for others the lover remains a secret from the partner. Who are we to moralise on such events in people's lives if we do not know all the circumstances and conditions?

We listen to the intimate stories of others. We do not rush to judgement. If appropriate, we ask questions. We encourage the person sharing their story with us to look deep into themselves. If the person wishes to hear our view of the situation, then we can offer it. A mutual inquiry can become a revelation.

The Duality of the Betrayer and the Betrayed

The so called duality of self and other deserves wholehearted attention and interest as our peace of mind and contentment of heart depends on the way we view the dynamics of a situation. We easily slip into harsh judgements on the behaviour of the other. I have experienced, on a couple of occasions, my partner developing an intimate relationship with another man while our relationship continued. The self–other thought can certainly gain some momentum in these circumstances. I recall a sense, a vague intuition, that my partner was hiding something from me. Some couples are willing to stay to try to work it all out. That can go on for months, even years. I tend to make a quick transition to a simple Dharma friendship. I feel it unwise to cut off deliberately all contact with the person in the aftermath of the ending of relationship as this means we cut off access to feelings within ourselves. There is the opportunity for a genuine friendship with the ex. Cessation of contact imparts far too much power from the seer (myself) onto the seen (my former partner). The change to Dharma friendship allows both people to move on without blame towards one another or oneself.

The knower, the known, the seer, and the seen function in the same way. There is an object of interest that gives rise to recognition. A man meets a beautiful woman or vice versa (or same gender). For example, attention and interest turn

153

towards the woman thus producing pleasurable sensations. (Sometimes the sight of the beautiful woman contrasts with the voice of the same woman so interest may drop away). The pleasurable sight and sound of the woman increases the level of interest producing particular sensations, the glow of warm sensations and pleasurable thoughts of what might develop.

From such recognition comes more attention and interest. It is at this point that the Buddha speaks of *sila* – virtue with an ethical communication. Is he or she ready to develop further contact? The pleasure of sight and sound of the woman can easily trigger *samkharas* (volitional tendencies) to increase the level of contact. If clarity, respect and sensitivity pervade the perception, then any subsequent action is in accordance with Dharma practice and free from questionable and unresolved volitional tendencies.

It is not unusual for a man or woman to tell themselves, and tell each other, that they wish only to develop a friendship and that is all. It is wonderful when this is the fact for both. If it is not, one person or the other will feel disappointed in the space of weeks or months. If there is any self-deception, then the volitional tendencies for sexual contact will arise generating pressure for the other person. It takes skill and calm to handle well the passions of energy. The Buddha referred to this cycle of ignorance (not seeing) leading to volitional tendencies, leading to desire and to the "whole mass of suffering." The repercussions of a single sexual encounter with a "friend" for whom attraction has developed can have unintended consequences that last for years, such as a growing distance between two people who were once close friends.

Over the years, I have spoken to numerous men and women whose volitional tendencies ruled their wisdom. "I went to bed with a man with whom I had become good friends. We suddenly found ourselves hugging and kissing. I

154

couldn't stop myself. I betrayed my partner. I told him. I had broken his trust. He was a very caring man. He left me. Five years later, I still feel ashamed. I showed no respect to myself, no respect to my partner and no respect to our relationship. "I lost my partner and I lost my best friend."

There are countless numbers of people living isolated lives while seeking friendships or a deep relationship. She or he may be looking for someone better for his or her lives. Why does the grass seem greener on the other side of the fence? There is no depth of lasting happiness, or deep contentment in all this. Fortunately, there are exceptions everywhere. There are caring and trustworthy people in the Sangha who would not risk causing another worry, agitation or suffering through their actions. They live with integrity and in a very caring way in their commitments. Such people are very dedicated in their personal and working lives.

The Buddha wisely gave much emphasis to respect for the feelings of another. The view of 'listening to my feelings' can become a reason to exploit a situation or take advantage of another's vulnerability. Purity of heart and clarity of mind takes priority over a decision to listen to one's feelings and act on them regardless of circumstances.

The Buddha said that vigilance remains a constant theme of the noble ones. Love is divine. Deep friendship is divine. The meeting of wisdom and intimacy serve as a liberating force from impulsive desire.

The wise know intimacy as clearly as knowing the intimacy of trees with wood.

Chapter 9

The Sangha and the Professional Session

When that painful feeling has arisen,
it invades his mind and remains because his mind is not developed.
MN 36.8

The divinity of love can seem far away at times. The heart can find itself catapulted into confusion, unhappiness and despair with regard to events of past, present or future when the presence of love has faded away. In such times, the Truth of such experience may not reveal the causes and conditions for it, except perhaps at an abstract level that does not transform the suffering. The one who is in such a plight then has to take steps to ensure wise counsel with another so that love, contentment and insight support the essential constitution of the inner life.

Both Dharma teachings and practices and psychotherapy have that task, offering similar and different approaches. Some find benefit with one kind of exploration and others find benefit with the other, or with both or neither. The Sangha of practitioners trusts in the power of the collective committed to a mutual depth of exploration to transform consciousness. The benefits of regular contact with like-minded seekers and the wise develop immense benefits for individuals and the group.

With the support of teachers and wise elders, the Sangha develops wisdom. This naturally reduces the stress, fears and anxieties without exaggerating or undermining their influence. The Sangha questions the so-called self, inwardly and outwardly, happy or unhappy, for a whole range of liberating insights and a deep sense of well-being.

There are two primary differences between the Dharma and psychotherapy as vehicles for the resolution of suffering.

- *Dharma practice offers a full training for a human being to address every major area of life in the process of waking up.*

- *Dharma addresses the formation of the "self." It questions the view 'this happens to me and that happens to me'. Dharma teachings say that this very view, often taken for granted in psychotherapy, is part of the problem.*

Most schools of psychotherapy and psychology generally appear to adopt the view that there is a *self*-experiencing a variety of conditions affecting the *self* in healthy and unhealthy ways. The Buddha never took the *self* for granted, never perceived the *self* as a given, as a fact, nor upheld its substantiality in any way. This is a critical difference between Dharma teachings and psychology. The inquiry into the construct of the *self* simultaneously challenges the view of who and what we think we are, and the construct of the world as we think it is.

It is not easy to follow through with such a teaching and exploration requiring a certain trust (as a form of love) that the Buddha knew what he was talking about. Love in such circumstances reflects as interest to find out about the apparent substantiality of the *self* and the insubstantiality of it. What are the conditions that seem to make the *self* something real and substantial and what shows its insubstantiality, its essential emptiness?

Dharma teachings make it clear that to even ascribe a personality to our *'self'* or to another *'self'* amounts to an

157

error of perception since it means grasping hold of perceived patterns or tendencies, and imposing a *'self'* upon them. There is neither truth, nor reality, to the view of 'having a personality,' or 'being unique' or 'we are all the same.' These views and beliefs arise dependent upon the grasping of the *self* and the other. They are all beliefs about the *self* in terms of body, feelings, perceptions, thoughts and consciousness. According to the Buddha, the notion of personality can arise in four ways. We believe at different times:

1. *I am the body, feelings, perceptions, thoughts or consciousness (identification)*

2. *I am in the body, feelings, perceptions, thoughts or consciousness (a self-residing within)*

3. *I am outside of body, feelings, perceptions, thoughts or consciousness (the witness to these five areas)*

4. *I am the owner of body, feelings, perceptions, formations or consciousness (a self who possesses body, my feelings etc.).*

When one view arises, it contradicts the other three in that moment. The Dharma does not support the notion of a separate *self*, a *self* that experiences oneness, a true *self* or a higher *self*. Who is making claim to these claims? Teachings of non-*self* and emptiness of I, me and mine, very rarely form part of the dialogue between therapist and client, although clients certainly can experience transformations in the process of therapy. Psychotherapy and psychology have a vitally important role to play in alleviating suffering, reducing problematic attitudes and relevant forms of behaviour. It is important to acknowledge, as well, the

158

discrepancies between the statements in the formal manuals of psychology and what actually takes place in the intimacy of sessions with the therapist. It is through the intimacy of the sessions that the real work of transformation takes place.

It may not be obvious, initially, that seeing the emptiness of the ego, or the emptiness of the formations of "I" and "my," has any direct relationship to love in its countless expressions. The one who meditates, the one who reflects and inquires with another, finds him*self* or her*self* charged with the task of dissolution of the ego, as it acts as a hindrance and obscuration to the liberation of love through the being.

The Buddha makes bold statements. He said: "*One who sees with clear wisdom dependent arising phenomena, it is impossible that he will run back into the past thinking:*

- *'Did I exist in the past?*
- *Did I not exist in the past?*
- *What was I in the past?*
- *How was I in the past?*
- *Having been that, what did I become in the past?'*
- *Or he will run forward into the future thinking:*
- *'Will I exist in the future?*
- *Will I not exist in the future?*
- *What will I be in the future?*
- *How will I be in the future?'*
- *Or will I be inwardly confused about the present:*
- *'Do I exist?*
- *Do I not exist?*
- *What am I?*
- *How am I?*
- *This being – where has it come from and where will it go?'*

- *The reason is seeing clearly with wisdom dependent arising and dependently arising phenomena."* (S. II. Book of Causation.20 (10)).

'Self' and 'Other' in Psychotherapy

Some types of psychotherapy offer a search for meaning for difficult experiences. Certain clients find it easier to work with suffering if they see some sound reasons for it. Other types may limit themselves to reducing compulsions and phobias. These forms of therapy can also bring great relief to clients who may have suffered years of personal torment. Therapy functions to change the meaning we give to such experiences. The change in the meaning can help clients come to terms with personal issues. The new meaning can dissolve anxiety, blame and other painful reactions to a situation.

The therapist or client may hold to the view that he or she has created all his or her own problems or that somebody else, past or present, caused them. The view that all problems are *self*-caused or caused by another or both is often a common social agreement. This view, itself, is problematic since it can feed blame. More and more the dynamics of psychotherapy focus on the present moment rather than focussing consistently on the past, or the family constellation in the past. It is not surprising that the approach of the Buddha and psychology find more and more common ground. The two disciplines have much to offer each other. The professional session offers the opportunity for much learning and understanding about the patterns of the 'self.' The client starts to see light in the dark.

I can offer a personal example of the benefits from engagement with psychology. I regularly visited over a period of six years (especially after I had a dream), a senior Jungian analyst living near my home in Totnes, England, to explore with him my 'blind spots', to bring out the depth of a dream and explore the place of Eros in the dynamics of human relationships. I have learnt much from these sessions.

I did not go to see the analyst because I experienced unhappiness or confusion but because I wanted to inquire further into the dynamics of the variety of relationships. I believe the benefits of these sessions have entered naturally into my role as a teacher, as much as other roles in my life. Other Dharma teachers have also benefited from contact with other practices. It is important to take every opportunity to develop as a human being to enable a full expression of freedom of heart and mind.

There is a deep element in our humanity that loves to explore.

Love and Relationship to Parents

Psychotherapy often addresses with the client the various projections and memories of the client around his or her parents, whether from childhood or in the current situation or both. The Buddha was not naive. He did not carry an idealist picture of parents. He remained very much aware of the failings and limitations of parents. He said that we can develop our capacity to offer trust if our parents are untrustworthy; we can develop morality if our parents are unwholesome, generosity if they are mean, or wisdom if they are unaware. The Buddha also recognised the value of loving parents. By inner development, he said, we can repay, or more than repay, our parents for their efforts.

To develop appreciation for the mother, a son or daughter reflects on the mother's pregnancy, the pain of giving birth and the mother's efforts to do what she could in the light of her own conditioning. Children can reflect on the

161

conditioning of the father. His conditioning affects his responses in terms of his role as a father, either through presence, absence or partial presence. Reflection into conditioning and consequences, a classic Dharma reflection, offers a far healthier approach than blaming parents for not giving enough love, or holding resentment towards them for their limitations or lack of presence. If there is some accuracy to a critical perception of parents, then the son or daughter can develop loving kindness and equanimity rather than harbour resentment about their upbringing. The same principle applies to others with whom there is a relationship.

The Buddha expressed a profound concern about holding to views regarding the causes of suffering. Psychotherapists could consider reading and re-reading the following words of the Buddha until deeply understood, if they are not already familiar with the analysis.

In the bamboo grove in the squirrel sanctuary in Rajghir, Bihar, the Buddha had an inquiry from an austere yogi belonging to another sect:

'Is suffering created by oneself?' the man asked the Buddha. The Buddha replied: 'Not so'

'Is suffering created by another?'
'Not so.'

'Is suffering created by both oneself and another?
'Not so.'

Does suffering arise by chance*?
'Not so,' said the Buddha.

'Is there no suffering? the man asked.

'It is not that I do not know and see suffering. I know suffering. I see suffering.' said the Buddha.

Then the yogi asked the Buddha for teachings on suffering.

Is suffering is caused by oneself?
The Buddha questioned whether the *self* who acts is the same one who experiences the result (eg. Is the child the same person as the adult? If so, this is a view of fixed continuity).

Is suffering caused by another?
The Buddha described this as an annihilationist view since it negates a possibility for inner change, for liberation since someone else is the cause of the problem. Blame stops resolution.

Is suffering caused by oneself and another?
(If so, what part of one and what part of another causes suffering?

If neither, then self and other have no responsibility whatsoever for any suffering that arises.)

The Buddha then explained that suffering occurs due to dependent arising conditions. It is not caused by any of the four propositions that the yogi made.

The yogi realised the Truth of what the Buddha said. *"The Dharma has been made clear showing the one to the way or holding the lamp for those with eyesight to see forms."* He responded with happiness. (S.11. Book of Causation 17.7)
*(**NB**. The Pali word for *chance* is *adhicca*. It also means *fortuitous, spontaneous, without cause, without reason, including belief in God's punishment.)*

163

The Buddha made a truly profound statement here. He unequivocally refuted the four standpoints that one*self*, another, both or chance cause suffering. Fault finding and blame mask over love expressed as the capacity to dwell in non-reactively to difficult circumstances. We show love in the form of respect for ourselves and others through not engaging in blame, vindictive behaviour and in an imperious way. Out of touch with love and equanimity, we can keep finding fault with ourselves and others that only confirms our incapacity to understand, and be at peace, with the causes and conditions that brought about suffering.

The Buddha went on to add: *"People maintain naively that pleasure and pain are created by oneself, by another, by both or neither by oneself nor by another."* This single dialogue and the Buddha's response constitute a radical shift away from the spell of perceptions, views and beliefs in *self*, other, both or neither as the cause for suffering. Problematic states of mind depend on belief in the spell of *self*. Realisation of the significance of the primary conditions for suffering, free from *self*-other grasping, changes the fundamental way of seeing life.

The Buddha said: *"Some people speak with malicious intentions. Others with the conviction they are right. The sage does not enter into controversy that has arisen as the sage is free from such mental constructions."* (Sn.780)

The Buddha spoke of the benefits of the Sangha and its importance in society. He said regularly that the Sangha is:

- *worthy of hospitality*
- *worthy of offerings*
- *worthy of respect*

- *and an unsurpassed field for merit.* (SN. Pge 319-321),

What does unsurpassed field of merit mean? Merit means the development of a positive potential for those who engage in kind actions to support the Sangha. The Buddha said we can regard the Sangha (the network of practitioners, the networks living with wisdom and compassion) as the best of groups to support to resolve suffering.

We can find such Sanghas in many walks of life.

Chapter 10

Tantra: Sex, the Arts and Life

The wise see action as it really has come to be.
They are proficient in the fruits of action. Sn. 653

As human beings, we are questioning creatures yet also prone to naïve beliefs, cultural indoctrination and an incapacity to look further afield than our immediate horizons. At times, our inquiry stretches far into the distant past. We can draw upon texts written many centuries ago. We find ancient views in psychology, philosophy, religion and science. The wise application of ancient teachings to the present situation comes first, rather than looking into history for its own sake. There is a capacity to draw upon the wisdom of the past, and discern the wisdom from whatever is outdated and irrelevant.

We have to look further afield, dig deeper to squeeze the honey out of ancient spiritual traditions that make a significant contribution to opening up our heart, our creativity and a liberating vision. The significance of Tantra is a case in point. It is frequently neglected, rejected or misunderstood. Tantra has something truly significant to offer the West when gleaned of various misconceptions, shadows and hostile attitudes. Tantra has endured much controversy owing to questionable elements and interpretations, but those free from such interpretations can examine the benefits of Tantra. Tantra broken away from the orthodoxy of the Buddhist-Hindu tradition since it promoted renunciation and sexual abstinence as an important step towards liberation. Tantrics actively endorsed love making and artistic creativity as vehicles for liberation. Their approach shocked the religious conservatives, the monks and yogis of India.

166

The image of the authentic and liberating tradition of Tantra has suffered for centuries due to the projections of certain Christian missionaries, hijack by sex-obsessed Westerners and abuse by violent worshippers of Kali. The original spirit and vision of the Tantra has been immersed in philosophical analysis, religious rituals and an aura of secrecy. It is time for Tantra, itself, to be liberated from the distortions of history, East and West, and from the reduction to scholarship of analysis of ancient Tantric discourses, Buddhist and Hindu. It is time to take the best of Tantra and apply it to daily life.

Christian missionaries, during the time of the British Raj, have to take some responsibility for the distortion of Tantra, which they regarded as a violation of human sensitivities, breaking every social taboo and convention of morality. This distortion is far away from the Truth, or at best, a jaundiced selection of weird rites, rituals and sacrifices by a tiny minority of followers. It has left a long-standing impression that Tantra represents a very dubious, if not dangerous, form of spirituality.

The second wave of interpretation of Tantra in the 20th century in the West exclusively associated Tantra with sex. Tantra meant sacred sex and became associated with workshops to develop sexual relationships/techniques to couples new to each other engaging in performing sexual practices. The name 'Tantra' legitimised using sex as a spiritual activity. Sacred sex certainly has a connection with historical Tantra in the same way that the genitals have a connection with the rest of the body but does not represent the whole. Tantric workshops have tended to ignore the whole teaching of Tantra and concentrate exclusively on the sexual component, while thoughtful and sensitive Tantric workshops have brought considerable benefit to participants' sexual lives. Wider Tantra teachings endeavour to show

Tantra as a way of life and not limited to any specific area of life.

Tantra expresses a diverse, complex spiritual approach to daily life, standing out from mainstream religion and spiritual orthodoxy. Tantra genuinely takes into consideration the important significance of energy, sensuality, human nature, our relationship to the body and its application, such as use of mudras. Mudras refer to the use of hands as symbolic gestures to show experiences, such as one hand resting on top of the other to show the mind of meditation or the tips of the thumbs touching with folded hands to show the experience of oneness with life.

Tantra also encourages forms of sacred art representing the constructive and destructive cycles of life, great and small. As a symbolic statement, a mandala can show itself through the arts. It takes sustained mindfulness, moment to moment concentration and artistic perceptions. Probably, the best known mandala is the sand mandala, painstakingly put together by Tibetan Buddhist monks over weeks, and then dissolved with a few sweeps of the hand.

We live in the field of arising and passing. This is a visual teaching reminding us that what forms together will dissolve, such as the mandala swept away in the movement of the hand.

According to Tantra, divine cosmic energy radiates through the body, the hands and sacred art in the process of waking up humanity.

The spirit and letter of Tantra sent shock waves through the established Buddhist-Hindu faiths in the 2nd- 3rd century. The orthodox religions of India kept strict divisions of seekers of Truth from wandering yogis to householders who kept precepts, made merit and supported the yogis. Religious beliefs adopted the view that only the yogis, monks and nuns could fully wake up and know liberation. Tantrics

168

(followers of Tantra) barely concerned themselves with this classification of householders/yogis since Tantra embraced energy, sensuality/sexuality, the arts and also pointed to an indivisible spiritual awakening. Tantrics applied male/female practices in real terms for householders and symbolic terms for celibate yogis. Male/female became archetypes for non-duality or wisdom and compassion, transcendence and imminence.

The tradition came to be called Tantra because it "elaborates" (tan) on reality (Tattva) to establish what amounts to a spiritual science. Tantra means "to weave, to expand and to spread." With its revolutionary impulse, Tantra turned religious practices on their head and helped bring in a golden age of spirituality in India from the 3rd century for the next five hundred years. The elaboration on spiritual practices, the strong affirmation of the arts, mythology and stories for realization and waking up, gave authentic Tantra a significant relevance in terms of establishing a new form of spirituality.

Utterly different from Western religion, Tantra today offers a radical alternative to Western religions as well as some of the stultifying forms of Eastern religions. With its revolutionary impulses, Tantra has much to offer the Western mind-set with its interest in the integration of energy, science, love, sex and cosmic life.

Rather than try to transcend desire and pleasure, a constant theme in the Buddhist Hindu tradition, Tantra endorses a different kind of approach that seeks to utilise desire and sensuality as a tool for awakening rather than as an obstacle. In the formation and development of the Tantric tradition, the practitioners responded strongly to this approach as it fully included sexual intimacy rather than pursuit of its transcendence. Tantra gave a meditative attention to life and death, male and female, devotion and

169

creativity. Depicting the Hindu gods, Tantric adepts cultivated stories and art forms. They took inspiration from the active romantic/sexual lives of the gods and goddesses, especially Siva and his consort, Parvati, who engage in a creative and passionate dance as one expression of their divinity.

Tantrics developed skilful means (*upaya*) to share together their sexuality as an expression of cosmic energy and cosmic oneness, while yogis employed mantras, visualisation practices, mandalas and the breath to harmonise the energies of heart, mind and body, romantic, sexual or otherwise. Instead of resistance to sensual energies, they welcomed them as a contribution towards the energising of consciousness. It was a radical change of attitude from what generations of gurus told their disciples and Buddhist abbots had told their monks and nuns.

Tantric Masters offered initiations (*diksha*) and empowerment (*abhiseka*). The free spirited attitude of Tantra meant that it was not necessary to identify with a particular Tantric guru in the quest for liberating Truth. For example, the Buddhist Tantric guru Naropa told his adepts: *"If, however, one happens to have a teacher who has no real knowledge and causes doubts, no harm would be incurred by leaving him. Indeed, as a bee eager for honey flies from flower to flower, so the practitioner eager for knowledge goes from master to master."*

A ninth century master, Naropa studied discourses of the Buddha and Tantra at Nalanda University in northern India until he left to go on a spiritual search outside the corridors of learning. Eventually, he found his teacher, Nilopa, with whom he underwent numerous spiritual hardships during his 12 years with him. In the Vajrayana tradition of Buddhism, regarded as the Buddhist Tantric tradition, Buddhists fondly remember Naropa for his unwavering devotion to Nilopa with both of them acknowledged as Tantric Masters of the monastic tradition.

The initial purpose of the initiation (*diksha*) introduced the practitioner to knowledge, rituals and the community of Tantrics who regarded themselves as representing *agama* - meaning without adherence to *nigama* (the orthodoxy of tradition such as the Vedas). The body of Tantric literature is *agama* ("that which has come to us") which addresses a variety of spiritual themes. Many Westerners engaged in Dharma practice in the West today would regard themselves as belonging to the *agama* tradition. They have little interest in the orthodoxies of the Vedas and prefer the discourses of the Buddha (*Sutta Nikaya*) which Indian scholars would regard as *agama,* as well as the yoga sutras. While most people in India remained loyal to the *nigama* tradition, Tantric practitioners always remained a minority; they were viewed as an esoteric sect, essentially upholding a non-traditional, non-orthodox philosophy of life.

Agama addresses four primary Paths:

1. *Spiritual knowledge from ancient non-Vedic texts, the oral tradition and contemporary wisdom* teachings.

2. *Yoga - inner discipline, postures, mudras, meditation, practices.*

3. *Art - the construction of temples, sculpture, carvings and paintings, including the erotic.*

4. *Rituals, festivals and pilgrimages*
    .

Tantra and Sexuality

Tantrics offer an important perspective on the place of sexuality in spiritual exploration, non-duality and the search for Truths that liberate consciousness from dis-ease with sexuality. Rather than flee from the sexual experience, they embraced the fusion of sexual energies through creative and artistic acts of lovemaking to include words, sounds and a wide variety of postures while making love. Adepts, one of the names used for Tantric masters, showed that lovemaking, passionate, energetic and adventurous, reflected the communion of cosmic energy.

No wonder Tantrics were often viewed as heretics to conservative Buddhists and Hindus! Emboldened to question religious standpoints around sex, Tantrics created sculptures of graphic sexual art in various temples in India as well as erotic art for the home, such as a statue of a naked dakini sitting in the lap of the Buddha. The act of making love had finally gained a spiritual significance. The voice of Tantra still resonates today among those of the *agama* tradition, who regard the separation of lovemaking and celibacy as a false hierarchical divide, having no relationship whatsoever to the religious impulse or spiritual development.

Tantric Texts

Tantric texts offer teachings that the reader can take on different levels as both actual and metaphorical. Myths, legends and stories, ancient and modern, were written to give access to the depths of the inner life rather than remain fixed in analysis, logic and rational thought. At first glance, a text translated from the Sanskrit may seem incomprehensible to the literal-minded but may offer insights from another level of the inner life. The esoteric nature of certain texts makes them extremely elusive even for the most seasoned Tantric adept. Some readers of ancient texts find they come back to a particular text weeks, months, years or decades and find a whole new meaning in an ancient discourse. There is the transformation of the incomprehensible to an understanding of certain texts, *nigama* and *agama*. *Mantras* (the repetition of a particular phrase or word that vibrates deep within to establish a pervasive calmness throughout the whole being) and *yantras* (symbols and geometric shapes often squares, triangles and circles revealing forms that lead to the centre) are recorded in Tantric texts. A text may contain lines of poetry to remind the practitioner of the importance of love, of intimacy.

> *"There is no end*
> *to the bliss of Madana's bewitcher.*
> *Lying lazily under the woman's hold,*
> *he thirsts for the taste of love place*
> *saying endearing things*
> *he makes love to the beautiful one*
> *in the lotus heart of Kamalakanta"*
> (Sayama Sangit no 131).

The *Sayama Sangit* is a 13th century Bengali love song dedicated to the goddess Kali. *Sayama* refers to her skin colour, often black.

In the *Kularnava* (the Ocean of Kula) Tantra is based on the 21,600 breaths a human being is said to take on a daily basis. The place of the heart serves as an essential aspect of Tantra.

"In other Paths, if one is a yogi, then one cannot be an enjoyer of life. Nor can one who enjoys life be a yogi. The path gives enjoyment of life and yoga and so it is greater than all other Paths.

173

The knowledge of the heart shines in one whose consciousness is pure, peaceful; whose actions serve the guru, who is extremely devoted, and can keep a secret.

The one who dwells within the heart is a vessel of enjoyment and liberation.

One who experiences the bliss of union in sexual relationship, as between the supreme power and the self, such a person knows the meaning of sexual relations.

Just as the divine couple are inseparable; just as the goddess Lakshmi is inseparable from Narayana and Saraswati from Brahma.

Body is the abode of God. I am He. The experience of bondage to one's animal nature is how one thinks of the embodied self. Liberated from this animal nature identity, one has the experience of the ever abiding Siva.

There are no commands. There are no prohibitions. There is no heaven and truly no hell for the followers of the heart.

Living anywhere, taking on any disguise and living and recognised by everyone in whatever social position he or she may be, he or she remains a heart Yogi."

Tantra confirms the unorthodox as a real path to total realisation. The essential doctrine of Tantra places worldly experiences firmly in the service of awakening rather than as a hindrance. Wise application of spiritual and worldly enjoyments, heaven and earth, serves as vehicles for access to insights, realisations and liberation. The Tantra tradition recognises the place of poetry, music, sacred dance, theatre,

174

meditation, sensuality and intimacy with spiritual depths – a revolutionary alternative to commandments, tight forms and beliefs of conventional religion. Currently, there is an exaggerated emphasis on meditation and mindfulness in daily life among many Buddhists so that far too many Westerners judge their spiritual development through a narrow prism. It is time to adapt the diversity of spiritual exploration of Tantra to Western culture, while leaving behind in the East the elements of Tantra with its secret initiations, rituals and shadowy history.

Tantrics learn to release their vitality and energy to enable the transformation of consciousness. Through a conscious engagement with all the senses, eyes, ears, nose, tongue and touch, reality expands offering spiritual nourishment and depth. This employment of passion, love and energy gives Tantrics the capacity to touch upon divine and ecstatic experiences, lifting consciousness out of the mundane. The Tantrics employed the arts to elicit sensuality and shed light on life rather than reduce the arts to a form of temporary entertainment.

Tantrics see life as a mandala of wondrous inter-active events emanating from the unformed.

One of the Indian Tantric texts bears the title *Garland of Gems,* a title that succinctly expresses the application and vision of Tantra. Tantric intimacy treats sexuality and the arts as belonging to a divine path. The Tantric embraces Siva and Shakti, lovers and single people, wisdom and love, yogis and yoginis, visionaries and healers. The thrust of Tantra empowers a variety of practices applied in imaginative and liberating ways, while drawing from or letting go of the cultural/religious background of participants.

Tantric texts refer to *going against the grain* of orthodox religious standpoints to explore the mandala of love, culture and spirituality. The Tantric adept offers initiations in

175

intimacy, sharing of heart, mind and body based on virtue and wisdom. These practises contribute to the integration of the fabric of daily encounters, offering fulfilment through weaving together the development of the senses and cultural depths to reveal essential Truth. Respected proponents of Tantra include Nagarjuna, the 3rd century Indian teacher who advocated the emptiness of *self*-existence.

Seven Chakras

The union of male and female serves as a metaphor and forms the union of wisdom and energy. The emphasis on transformation through meditation, insight and a different attitude takes priority, rather than the effort to renounce the mundane desires, personal needs and different forms of clinging. Tantrics acknowledge the risks of inflating the ego, or building a deluded view, through full engagement with every arena of life. They see the risk as worth taking because of the potential for a major breakthrough into an awakened life, expansive and inclusive.

Tantra adopted the meditative employment, application and practice of the *chakras* (wheels), regarded as the vital concentration of energy or life force. By focussing with calm and concentration on a chakra, the Tantric established its importance as step towards full awakening. The chakras serve to remind the practitioner of the primary areas of significance for a human being. The most common seven locations for *chakras* are:

1. *Crown of the head*
2. *Forehead between the two eyes*
3. *Throat*
4. *Centre of the chest*
5. *Solar Plexus*

6. Navel
7. Base of the spine

The crown chakra represents our relationship with the cosmos, the sky above, the night sky and the vast sense of it all. In this chakra, we sense the transcendent rather than the concerns of the self.

The Third Eye chakra represents consciousness. We often feel our so called "I" is located above and just behind the eyes from where we view the world. This chakra enables the clear seeing of the contents of the mind. Consciousness reveals the content, and content confirms consciousness.

The throat chakra represents speech. Our voice forms words, sounds, chants, mantras and songs that reach out to others, humans, animals and reptiles, and much else, as well as vibrate through our being.

The heart chakra represents our feelings, emotions, passion and love. We direct energy to this chakra to expand our heart to all, far and wide, including our life.

The solar plexus chakra represents energy, risk-taking, the power to act. We sometimes know we have to take a risk. We feel a sensation in the solar plexus. This is the wheel of the chakra struggling to turn.

The abdomen chakra represents food and sexuality. Although referred to by some as a lower chakra, it does not mean an inferior chakra. We need to give energy to a healthy diet, mindful eating with respectful expressions of sexuality and thoughtful views about making love.

The root chakra represents our connection to the earth, our sense of being, and our physicality. This chakra reminds us of the importance of matter, of the bare elements.

Although the *chakras* indicate a physical location, the Tantrics perceived each one of the *chakras* as an important element of psychological life and through directing meditative attention to each chakra that chakra gained a vital and divine energy. Every *chakra* has a place and significance to remind the practitioner of the vital importance of giving attention to every one of the seven *chakras* for a whole and balanced life. Any neglect of these wheels (*chakras*) that turn our life, brings about an unwise, unskilful application of energy with the agitation, confusion and suffering that go with such neglect.

A Tantric practitioner reflects on the significance of every *chakra* to know which ones he or she needs to develop, to meditate on in order to discover a genuine wholeness as a human being. The shift from isolation to the collective, from reader about Tantra to being in the company of practitioners helps ensure the turning of each wheel (*chakra*) to enable our life to move easily and freely.

There are teachers in the West who draw upon the *chakras* as explored in Tantra. There are teachers in the West who offer teachings on the release and application of energy as in Tantra. There are teachers who offer Tantra as exclusively a sexual practice. Tantra is also demonstrated in science when science expands our understanding and our sense of wonder. Traditional, modern and post modern art, whether sculpture, paintings, music, dance, poetry, literature, theatre and cinema, have an element of Tantra when the art form reveals to the audience, as well as the artists, insights and inspiration for our daily life. With its emphasis to elaborate, expand and weave together, Tantra recognises the gifts and creative practises that open out our consciousness.

Certain teachings, spiritual, religious, psychological and scientific, can concentrate and expand on one of the *chakras* from the top *chakra* (cosmic consciousness) down to the root *chakra* (intimacy with the Earth). While welcoming the specialisation of the different wheels of *chakras*, as a tangible reminder of what matters, few exponents of Tantra can embody the wealth of Tantric teachings, whether monks, nuns, yogis or householders. An eager bee may have to fly from flower to flower, as Naropa commented, to draw upon the pollen. Such a seeker needs to keep a mindful presence in the face of teachers, teachings and centres. Seekers take note of their ethics, values, attitudes and charges for workshops or retreats.

Once again, Tantra emphasises the necessity for the Tantric to remember that what he or she perceives as a hindrance actually serves as vehicle for change, for integration. So there is no need for householders and yogis to cling to any identity as a householder or wandering yogi as they each have an equal opportunity to develop.

Some lamas in the Buddhist tradition of Tantra have offered secret texts to those initiated such as the *Guhyagarbha Tantra* with its "secret essence." Initiated ones might receive the empowerment of *"Vajrasattva's Magical Manifestation Matrix"* (regarded as Tantras of Enlightenment) in order to get to read the sacred book. It may be that the secrecy, often associated with Tantra, springs from its early origins through the exploration of physical intimacy on the Path of Practice. Core features of Tantra include:

- *action*
- *behaviour*
- *conduct*

- *initiations*
- *movement*
- *mudras*
- *performance*
- *rituals*
- *sexual union*
- *touch*
- *yoga*
- *and the Supreme Yoga (Yoga Niruttara - With No Higher).*

Tantra defies boundaries

Tantra essentially gives practitioners permission to explore outside the accepted parameters of what most people would regard as possible and permissible. Some people found it difficult to adjust to yogis who followed no particular discipline, no particular lineage, nor obeyed or subjected themselves to any particular precepts, rules or vows. A Tantric text from the Vajrayana tradition of the 18th century, *Laughter of the Dakinis*, reads:

> *"I, feeling this united, practising*
> *to unite Samsara and Nirvana,*
> *dancing on the deities and spirits of the ego*
> *reduced to dust the discursive thought of transmigration*
> *that generates dualities."*

The recorded practices of Tantra are primarily contained in ancient books, and a small number have been translated from Sanskrit to English. Some Tantrics wrote books that were unintelligible to the majority of its readers as these books accompanied the teachings of a Tantric master. Without the master, the books made little or no sense.

180

Buddhist and Hindu scholars generally agree that it is not possible to summarise Tantra owing to the diversity of approach to numerous aspects of spiritual exploration. Tantra leaves few stones unturned in the spiritual life although it lacks a political and global perspective.

The relationship of the *guru* and *sādhaka* (spiritual practitioner) forms an important connection in Tantra due to the combination of trust based on evidence of the wisdom of the Guru, and trust based on evidence in the aspirations and determinations of the *sādhaka*. A *sādhaka* is one who follows a particular *sādhanā* (literally, 'the means to accomplish'). *Sādhaka, sādhanā* also relates to the word *sādhu*, derived from the verb root *sādh* - 'to accomplish'. One who has not yet accomplished the goal of awakening is referred to as the *sādhaka* while one who has reached the goal is known as a *siddha*. Generations of Buddhist *sādhaks* referred to the Buddha as Gautama *Siddhartha*: Gautama the Accomplished One.

Feminine principles and energy influenced the original conceptions and development of Tantra through equal recognition of the goddesses, a non-patriarchal approach to spirituality, the unity and non-duality of gender, with stories and art forms that expressed equality between men and women, gods and goddesses. As mentioned in another essay, Siva sat in the cave in the full lotus in deep meditation. Parvati, the Queen of the Himalayas, sat in exactly the same position in front of Siva, a *sādhu* (ascetic). Siva did not try to send her away so he could remain as a solitary yogi (unlike the Buddha) but welcomed her into his cave. This historical/mythological event launched the intimacy of Siva and Parvati. The dancer and the dance (Siva and Parvati, wisdom and skilful means, knowledge and compassion) became one.

Since Tantra fails to fit any kind of simple categorisation, it seems elusive in terms of trying to give a definition to Tantra as it defies boundaries. Given the common Western use of the word "Tantra" around sacred sex, it is time for the rehabilitation of the broad approach to spirituality that marks Tantra. While making use of ancient *agama* texts, Tantra continues to be primarily an oral tradition with teachers selecting aspects of Tantra to espouse upon for the welfare of the *sādhaks,* and offering full inclusion of the body in spiritual practice through diet, sexuality, physical presence and cellular makeup. Tantrics give loving attention to the energy in all their cells and sub-atomic particles. They treat the cells as a divine element capable of revealing light and enlightenment.

Via meditation and yoga, Tantric practitioners gained access to kundalini energy, often referred to as the coiled serpent or coiled power. In the depth of calm, through the diminishing of tension and stress, the cells release energy that travels through the body to enhance the entire being and consciousness. Like a current of electricity, kundalini energy can move through the body to generate all manner of states of mystical experiences, shifts of consciousness and visions. The 'reality' of the usual view of the world may find it*self* supplanted with a new view just as real in appearance as the previous version of reality.

The guidance of the wise master matters in Tantra, especially for sexuality, *chakras* and *kundalini* practices. Otherwise seekers run the risk of stimulating mental turmoil through inexperience or using will power to achieve results and thus generating dangerous levels of pressure. The inner life can link energies of heart, mind, body and consciousness. This requires skill and appropriate methodology to experience the direct benefits of such expressions of Tantra. This requires the guidance of the adept.

With virtuous conduct as an indispensable factor, energy, sexual intimacy, *chakras* and *kundalini* energy can harmonise together for profound experiences of our human capacities, often ignored and neglected. Love confirms a subtle and powerful energy that contributes with skilful practices and insight, to the dissolution of gross behaviour and blocked energy including negative and fearful energies.

A skilful *sādhanā* contributes immensely to finding our way into the heart of Tantra while an unskilful *sādhanā* can drive a person into madness. Tantra requires vigilance and empathy with one*self* and others to safeguard all from confusion and disorder. We develop Tantra to establish a profound sense of wellbeing, harmony with the rhythms of life, a healthy lifestyle and direct knowing of liberation amidst the cosmic dance. Tantra reminds us of the way life expands, contracts and weaves together.

A rehabilitated Tantra has much to offer Western life. Tantra has the capacity to wake us up from the dream of habitual life, challenge clinging to fixed norms and release a creative and liberated passion.

Chapter 11

The Act of Compassion Reveals our Humanity

*One insight reveals that feelings and sensations
is the basis of all suffering. Sn 738*

In its June, 2013 issue, TIME magazine, the US weekly news publication, pictured Burmese monk Venerable U Wirathu Ashin on its international cover with the headline 'The Face of Buddhist Terror.'

In a direct reference to Burmese Muslims, the Buddhist monk has said: "You can be full of kindness and love, but you cannot sleep next to a mad dog. I call them (Muslims) troublemakers because they are troublemakers," he claimed.

Venerable U Wirathu Ashin has repeatedly called upon Burmese Buddhists to unite against Muslims. He claims Muslims "breed too fast and have hijacked the business community." His inflammatory statements seem to have contributed to fierce anti-Muslim sentiment with more than 200 deaths, mostly of Muslims, as well as the torching of a mosque and Muslim orphanage in the north east of Burma.

The UN described the Rohingya Muslims as one of the most persecuted minorities in the world. They were originally immigrants, brought into Burma by the British at the time of the British Raj as cheap labour. They have lived in Burma for 200 years.

These painful incidents in Buddhist countries only serve to remind thoughtful people that being in possession of a religion, such as Buddhism, gives no assurance of the expression of compassion. These exceptions include a small number of lay Buddhists and a handful of Burmese Buddhist monks, who continue to endorse these violent attacks on the

Muslim minority. The ethnic violence in Burma sent shockwaves through the West since many assumed that all Buddhists, especially monks, practiced nonviolence, mindfulness and compassion as the very foundation and essential principles of the religion.

The worldwide media attention showed how violence can take a hold on consciousness despite a 2600-year-old Buddhist philosophy of living in harmony and emPathy with others. As the Buddha commented:

"One does not take up the weapon to inflict suffering on others."

It is the first training rule, the major precept, and the recognition that the deliberate taking away of another person's life expresses the most grievous of all human actions.

The Buddha added: *"Do not learn the Dharma for the sake of criticising others. The teachings are conducive for the welfare and happiness of all. If a man grasped a snake by the tail, he would come to suffering."* (MN 22.3)

U Wirathu Ashin, has gained international name and fame after he called himself the Burmese Osama Bin Laden, but notoriety stands far removed from compassion, far removed from speaking for the welfare and happiness of others.

The violent incidents in Burma remind us of the necessity to make clear that compassion functions as a direct act to dissolve suffering. Buddhism has its shortcomings in terms of such action even though the religion, to its credit, makes frequent reference to compassion. Those with a deep understanding of the Buddha's message endeavour to live with compassion for others above personal desires.

Buddhist monasteries have often acted as an oasis of peace in Buddhist countries. They provide a haven of safety for people in cities, towns and villages in difficult times. People suffering under violence, terrorism, drug addiction and alcohol issues will take refuge in the monastery. Yet, occasionally, monks can use the quiet of the monastery to sow seeds of doubt and conflict in the minds of other monks, nuns and lay visitors. In the quiet atmosphere of the monastery, politeness and deference often matters more than questioning of attitudes and prejudices. Laypeople hold monks in such high regard that they would be unwilling to question even the most obnoxious views. U Ashin joined the monastery at 16 years of age as an ordained novice and then he took full ordination four years later. It is hard to imagine that he never expressed his Islamaphobia in the monastery.

- *Did his fellow monks, teachers and abbot ignore him?*
- *Did he crave attention so much that his mind had to create the "other" to draw attention to himself?*
- *Does his ego have a narcissistic complex with the need to be the centre of attention?*
- *Is he craving respect at the expense of the vulnerable Muslim community?*
- *Is he a verbal bully?*

The consciousness of U Wirathu Ashin's years in a monastery, as well as years in prison for his hatred of Muslims, remains in the spell of his conviction in belief in us (Buddhists) and them (Muslims). There is a bizarre irony in that he proudly boasts that he is Burma's Bin Laden. Hasn't anybody told the monk that Bin Laden had a Muslim background? U Ashin's psychology mirrors the mind set of those who perceive blame lies with the others, rather than examine causes and conditions for suffering. We confirm compassion through inquiry into the conditionality for suffering and response to it.

Meditation and Compassion

Meditators need to question themselves whether their meditation practice offers inspiration and insight in terms of the transition from the cross legged bearing, to compassion.

- *Is there any significant causal relationship between meditation and compassion?*
- *If so, what is it?*
- *Does the journey of inwardness bear a significant, little or no relationship to compassion?*
- *What is the most fertile ground for compassion to express in all directions?*

Thought, word and deed collectively confirm compassion rather than sitting on the cushion meditating on warm, loving feelings towards oneself and others. This kind of "compassion" on the cushion belongs essentially to the feel good factor for meditators who perceives a positive state of mind as an expression of Dharma practice as distinct from a negative state of mind.

Dharma reveals it*self* in its unwavering endorsement of the transformative power of a human being to open up consciousness, reveal depths of experience and generate love and compassion in all directions. Certain Buddhist teachers teach loving kindness and compassion meditation for one*self* and then compassion for others. These meditations certainly enhance deeper intimations of the heart to arouse a certain concern for one*self* and others, near and far, but such experiences become confused with real compassion that expresses as direct, meaningful action.

Genuine compassion only has meaning in the action to resolve suffering through changing the causes and conditions that make the arising of suffering possible. This principle of inquiry into suffering and its causes applies everywhere, including to the systems and ideologies that contributes to suffering as well as the personal experiences of suffering. Compassion includes the persons who suffer and tackles the structures that perpetuate suffering. We can describe the practice of loving kindness and compassion on the cushion as 'compassion light.'

Sadly, Buddhism has a long-standing history of belonging to the 'cult of the cushion,' namely sitting cross-legged meditating, chanting or listening to teachings as a lifestyle, rather than a preparation for the active engagement of compassion for humans, animals and the environment. Buddhists coined the term 'engaged Buddhism' in the 1970's to remind Buddhists and others of the significance of compassion in the field of human existence. We practice to develop the wisdom to act with compassion to deal with any dynamic triggering suffering. There is the regular return to the meditation cushion for renewal before re-entering into the heat of situations.

Countless numbers of monks, the tiny number of ordained women as nuns, and lay people, East and West, spend an inordinate number of hours engaged in chanting and meditating. Chanting compares to reading out loud the instructions from the Buddha on a box of medicine without actually taking the medicine. The chant gives a certain peace of mind yet, at the same time, gives confirmation of a disengagement from the world. Chanting in monasteries can absorb hours every day for the residents. This ritual has little, if anything, to offer people and animals suffering in the world. The memorisation and repetition of passages from ancient texts give precious little inspiration for insight to apply changes to our world.

There are noticeable exceptions, but few Buddhists find empowerment via meditation to make compassion the highest priority in their lives. With so much emphasis on meditation, the cushion then has a magnetic pull as a sure way to distance oneself from the world and abide temporarily in a certain cocoon of comfort or become absorbed in the struggles, physical and mental, of the *self*.

The actual movement of compassion confirms a depth of embodied and instinctive sensations in the core of our being that makes us respond to the plight of suffering, even, at times, at personal risk. Authentic compassion reveals itself as a precious force in the cells of our being, pleasant or uncomfortable. We continue to worship, rightly so, the gods of history who have displayed immense love and compassion for others, even at the cost of their own lives. The proof of their inspiration shows itself when we act with compassion, not in our devotion and adulation of the gods of history.

What is a fertile ground for compassion? It is men and women meeting together to explore an issue with a determination to find the skilful means (*upaya*) to act to end suffering. The Sangha of practitioners, large or small groups, organises activities to take the necessary steps. Numerous examples of compassionate initiatives within Buddhism in the West include the creation of monasteries, spiritual centres, mind/body/spirit programmes, classes, workshops, retreats and endless acts of service to others for their welfare and benefit. Lovers of the Dharma feel a willing obligation to give equal support to family and friends, accompanied also with a deep instinctive response to the needs of others including strangers and hostile individuals/groups/nations. That is empathy. That is compassion.

At face value, compassion would seem to be rooted in an essential dualism of *self* and other. The view might be: "I meditate, I give loving kindness to my*self*, I send compassion to my*self*. After I have developed enough compassion for my*self*, I share my compassion with others." This dualistic view of *self* first and others second assumes a reality of *self* and a reality of *self* separated from another. Language with its metaphors and various turns of speech, reinforces the duality. This deeply entrenched notion, if not ideology, stands in marked contrast to the Buddha's teachings on non-*self*. The release of the instinctive sensation of compassion from the depth of being requires insights into the fictionalised viewpoint of a *self* called "I" and a *self* called "you." This duality in perception and language obscures natural, instinctive compassion free from such duality.

We have to keep faith and trust in the Four Truths of the Noble Ones, namely

1. Suffering.
2. Causes/conditions for suffering
3. Complete Resolution.
4. The Way to the resolution.

Some practitioners live in a 'wish washy' world of slavish repetition of Buddhist one-liners, such as 'I take a vow to save all sentient beings" - a fairy-tale view that only the ego could dream up in the guise of a well-meaning intention. Other practitioners address suffering in the specific and the detail with a willingness to be direct, questioning and fearless, in communication rather than avoid issues or slip into unworldly generalisations.

Buddhism suffers from its own history through the constant repletion of stories and analogies that, upon hearing, we nod our head with approval but in the long term, it has

190

little effect. For example, we have heard on countless occasions that for a bird to fly, it requires two wings; so for the Dharma to fly, it requires two wings – one of wisdom and one of compassion. Yes, yes. The reminder goes out. It can provide a little inspiration for those who hear the analogy for the first time but then it becomes merely a pleasing turn of speech.

Inner Transformation and Compassion

Contemporary Buddhist practices have an underlying flawed view that inhibits the meeting of wisdom and compassion, namely an internalised, privatised, psychological interpretation of suffering, often bound to an attitude that *self* comes first, or to the repetition of a meditation technique. Clinging to a technique of meditation, or clinging to being in the present moment, will inhibit a liberating inquiry into the contingency factors for experiences.

There is an accompanying belief that if I, the meditator, change then I change the world. I believe I have to work on my*self* first, purify my mind, find inner peace and stillness, and only then will I be ready to offer compassion to others and to the world. This view of *self* and other shows a naivety about true reality, unless we take for reality our habitual thinking and linguistic conclusions about the way things are. An ongoing negligence of inquiry into the emptiness of view of *self* and other, in and out of meditation, reinforces the duality to the point that we cannot perceive in any other way. The duality fuels an unhealthy and unnecessary fragmentation of mind, a divided perception instead of seeing into the notion of "I" and "my" or "you" and "yours."

Some will view a profound spiritual/religious experience as enlightenment. The experience then gives some the authority to offer teachings. Based on first-hand experience, such teachings can point out a way or approach that is genuinely helpful in daily life. The same teachings may express major limitations despite the efforts of the teacher to point to the limitless Truth. Again, there is little evidence to show that such profound experiences provide the transformed person with the knowledge, skills, insights or abilities to address the extent of problems found, for example, in the family as well as in social, political, financial, environmental or global matters. Yet countless numbers listen with rapt devotion to the spiritual masters, Buddhist and others, and their accounts of their *self* transformation, while overlooking the limits of their enlightenment experience.

We do not have to doubt the personal reports of the transformational experience. The lives of such people are certainly enhanced through such experiences in their private, inner world. They may exude inner peace, the power of attention and a charismatic presence, but that does not mean to say the guru, the master, the teacher, the lama or the ajahn has a clue about the necessary wisdom and compassion to attend to the suffering in public issues such as abortion, animals' rights, climate change, consumer goods, corrupt banks, energy crises, environmental degradation, euthanasia, food, globalisation, human rights, multi-nationals, obscene wealth, poverty, travel, war and much more. The spiritual teacher may lack the wisdom and insight to shed light on the family constellation, the inter-personal dynamics at work, the conflict between partners and skilful ways to handle problematic children.

We might believe that a profound inner shift will give us the skills and empowerment to change the mind of others. This belief borders on futility, a perversity of view with the power of the *self* given supremacy. The subsequent application of mindfulness, insights and skilful application contributes to personal and social change. The Buddha regularly came back to the examination of the Four Noble Truths of suffering, its causes and conditions, its resolution and the way to the resolution. One hears, from time to time, from Buddhist meditators "If everybody meditated, then everybody would be at peace with each other...." or words to that effect. Such a view falls into unrealistic and idealistic thinking as if residing in the narrow internalised world will answer global issues, great and small.

The meditator can end up adopting a position that being a mindful and calm serves as the goal of Dharma practice, rather than realisations about all four Noble Truths and their application everywhere and to everything. Some Buddhists find fault with those who work to transform institutions, social, corporate and political, because activists do not work on themselves. Other Buddhists will talk and write about the illusion of separation. Other Buddhists will prioritise being mindful in the moment and see this as a spiritual achievement. Yes, the world appears different when attraction and aversion, likes and dislikes lose their capacity to distort perception. One then inhabits a different world, a parallel universe, so to speak, compared to previously when living under the spell of personal problems and hindrances. The one who has experienced such a transformation knows inner peace, but that inner peace does not ensure compassionate action.

Dharma includes the disciplines of mindfulness and meditation in the postures of sitting, walking, standing and reclining, one to one consultation with the teacher and listening to teachings in the Dharma hall to provide an excellent therapy, a resource for insights into personality issues and a deep sense of well-being. Some will actively keep in mind the potential for enlightenment while others will see primarily in terms of psychological well-being. In either case, compassion will not necessarily take a high priority.

The concerns about lacking the development of compassion do not finish here. Some practitioners have taken on board the problem of the seeing the *self* separate from others. The view of separation seems to be a major problem, since in the vast scheme of things, there is no separation. Others say the dissolution of the apparent separate *self*, gradually or suddenly, reveals the true reality as oneness. Again, these views seem to bear little relationship to compassion.

Once you exercise the freedom to engage with the everyday world, while, at the same time, knowing the world undistorted through greed, negativity and delusion, you will find your*self* attending directly to the Four Noble Truths including the skilful means to resolve suffering. You will probably be in contact with others who know the world anew through their realisations. You will probably be in contact with those with the knowledge, insights and skilful means to act compassionately to change the dynamics of a situation. Those people or groups may, or may not, have the knowledge and skills to work on themselves. They may have a different analysis of problems, offering a different perspective on the wise way forward that your profound spiritual awakening did not reveal in that moment. A genuine awakening punctures the ego leaving a genuine humility to bring us closer to others and to the Earth.

It is too easy for Buddhists to hold to the view that changing the *self* matters first and foremost. Logical thinking supports this view. "First I save my*self* from my *self* and then I do the same for you or tell you that you have to save your*self*." Those with wisdom advocate ethics, sustainable lifestyle and the importance of the company of the wise. Compassion is a *self*less language. If the *self* says: "I am a compassionate person," it ought to cause concern for the listener to such a claim because it sounds conceited, even arrogant. Selflessness enables compassion to respond to the process, to what unfolds both sentient and insentient. There is an instinctive free movement of love to resolve suffering. There is nothing patronising about it, such as "I am doing this out of compassion for you." The hand naturally reaches down to the shin when we bruise it. The hand does not think "I, the hand, am doing this for you, the shin." It is a natural movement expressing the process of necessity.

Nirvana and Compassion

If the meditator does not use the Dharma as a tool for psychological improvement, he or she may grasp onto meditation to reach the metaphysical (beyond the physical) conceived of as Nirvana, the Unmanifest, the Unconditioned. This view also keeps the meditator on the cushion with a common view that desire, clinging and identification with mind and body inhibit the realisation of Nirvana. Consciousness finds it*self* in the spell of this second common view, one also that Buddhist teachers often propound. Some teachers react against this view, and to quote a famous one line from an ancient Buddhist text that, 'compassionate beings (*bodhisattvas*) renounce Nirvana to save all sentient beings.' This places bodhisattvas in the very awkward position of pointing the way to Nirvana as the resolution of suffering, without actually knowing and seeing Nirvana in these circumstances. Bodhisattvas do not then have the authority to speak about that which they reject.

The view of striving for Nirvana makes it extremely difficult for the meditator to break free from his/her meditation techniques/methods/no methods and the object of meditation (such as Nirvana). The Noble Ones give priority to reflection and meditation on ethics, the power of meditative concentration (on and off the meditation cushion) through application of the principles of the Four Truths of the Noble Ones. The Buddha dispensed with metaphysical ambitions, the inner versus the outer, so that seeing and knowing the Truth of a situation take priority. This view puts an end to the 'cult of the cushion' while leaving meditation concentration *(samadhi)* as an important link in the Eightfold Path, with one eighth of the significance of the path. It is useful to bear in mind that the Buddha designated *samadhi* as the last link in the Eightfold Path. In ancient India, *samadhi* took central priority for the yogis, while the Buddha gave immense significance to *samadhi* without exaggerating it above everything else. We develop *samadhi* to concentrate with clear comprehension on the welfare others.

Some meditators believe that their experience of oneness confirms their enlightenment. In spiritual terms, oneness refers to a state of wholeness, a sublime condition of harmony and unity. Beyond our individual differences, we can experience various levels of oneness, of non-separation of one person or thing from other. A deep experience of oneness transforms our perceptions. For example, the deep experience of oneness with others, near and far, may dissolve the desire to support war. The Buddha placed his emphasis on deep experiences to provide the necessary insights to attend to suffering, the causes and conditions, the resolution *(nirvana* means without fire) and the way. Absolute views on the metaphysics of Cosmic Consciousness, Universal Intelligence, The Now, God, the True *Self* and Transcendent Awareness seem far removed from the Buddha-Dharma of liberation through wisdom, love and insight into the dependently arising conditions.

This duality of here and beyond leads to spiritual tensions about the experience of the Absolute, the nature of it,

196

the way to it and whether this absolute is personal or impersonal. Some claim a path to the Absolute while others claim there is no path as the enlightenment experience just happens. They claim there is nothing that you can do to get closer to it. None of these spiritual issues about an Absolute indicate any obvious connection with compassion.

The dynamics of the human situation reveal far more complexity than sitting on the meditation cushion or Being in the Now or proclaiming some kind of absolute experience. There are dedicated spiritual teachers and meditators who have, under their belt, a wide variety of deep experiences and are calm, peaceful and remarkably stress free, yet take no account of the environmental cost of their daily behaviour, extravagant lifestyle and maximisation of pleasure/entertainment. The desire for the material world gives shape to consciousness, including meditators living in an ostentatious way.

Some dedicated people passionately engage in acts of compassion making a real difference to the world with neither the resources nor the time to work on themselves. They come to realise that nirvana reveals as the absence of a consciousness of greed, blame and delusion. This seeing and knowing of the absence of problems reveals the highest happiness, enabling compassion to flow in an effortless way. Mental hindrances and impure thoughts may not have the power to inhibit compassionate work. Pure hearted people, largely free from hindrances, developed inwardly through meditation, therapy, and other forms of mind/body work. Yet they can neglect the application of compassionate action, except perhaps in times of need for family members and friends. Others neglect the welfare of their inner life to engage in compassionate action. Nothing is clearly straightforward. Deep meditation and transcendent experiences do not guarantee compassion, likewise mental hindrances do not have to have the power to block compassionate action.

Meditation and Daily Life

A meditator genuinely welcomes a real depth of calmness and stillness, an untroubled state that remains, even when arising from the cushion. It is heavenly to be able to go through the variety of tasks of everyday life and not feel burdened at all with problems and various forms of unrest. This is the taste of Nirvana. People come on retreats at Buddhist centres and monasteries in the West to find such expressions of inner peace, often leaving the centre only to find that the peace they found lasts for no more than a few days. The duality of meditation retreats and daily life become a constant struggle for integration. It misses the point again. Dharma teachings do not exalt the reaching of a particular state of inner calm on the cushion and then holding onto it through the variety of daily tasks. It is an impossible dream, a false duality to resolve.

Yes, a change in consciousness matters, but not in order to reach a permanent state of balance but to find the wisdom and compassion to attend to the Truths of life. An equanimous state shows development along the path but is a long way short of a genuine awakening. Awakening provides the awareness and vitality to explore the skilful means to change the corruptions of consciousness on issues such as poverty, racism, corporate greed, globalisation and environmental destruction. All of these problems of our species have the underlying influence of greed, negativity and delusion. A peaceful mind certainly indicates an absence, for a period, of greed and negativity, but can reinforce delusion by exaggerating the importance of a calm being and inner stillness above all else.

If there is a departure from the integrity of the Four Noble Truths, then the seeker/meditator will give priority to personal experience above everything. Some will adopt a transcendent view beyond the world and its suffering. If the meditator has such an experience, he or she may conclude that the mind/body/world matters little, since it is a transitory event. The so-called enlightened person may feel little compassion for others or encourage others to pursue the same experience as themselves in the form of a transcendent enlightenment.

Mindfulness and Compassion

Buddhist meditators share certain deep experiences using similar and dissimilar views and interpretations of their experiences in secular/spiritual/religious language. Even with similar deep experiences, the same meditators may widely disagree with ways to attend to suffering in the world. They would surely be deluding themselves if they think for one moment that a temporary experience of oneness or sublime bliss is the ongoing solution to any manifestation of suffering.

Buddhists like to point out that anybody and everybody can benefit from mindfulness and meditation: a child, a patient, a criminal, a soldier, a depressed person, a company executive, a politician. Mindfulness reduces the level of stress and contributes to calmness which is clear, productive and efficient. That does not mean to say that mindfulness/meditation spills over naturally into looking into greed, hate and delusion. In fact, mindfulness can play a role in maintaining the status quo through not questioning the greed/results driven addiction of an executive, the aggression of a soldier or the addiction to power of a politician. This means that there is no change, while the political/corporate/educational powers can point to the tools of mindfulness to keep citizens/customers/students subservient to the ambitions of those with power. It takes compassion as well as strong determination, to question the corrupt mind and corrupt ideologies in the private and public sector.

There are numerous examples in the discourses of the Buddha of his determination to challenge the voices of authority, to make them examine their attitudes and behaviour.

The Buddha spent most of 20 years in the Anathapindika's Park in Savatthi, the capital of Kosala. King Pasenadi of Kosala attended regular meetings with the Buddha. In the Kosalasamutta in Samyuttta Nikaya, it is written that King Pasenadi of the Kosala kingdom approached the Buddha but he was surprised at his youthful appearance. "Master Gautama is so young in years" he commented.

The Buddha responded: *"There are four areas which one should not disparage or despise who or what is young – a king, a poisonous snake, a fire and a wise being."*

Without mincing his words, the Buddha then goes on to speak bluntly to the King. The Buddha spoke to the King directly about his behaviour on some 25 issues. The King's subjects knew that if the King worked on his greed, anger and delusion, they would all benefit. The people loved the Buddha for his fearless compassion and for not showing any special deference to their King. He gave King Pasenadi a warning about being careful with his actions.

Warning the king about the importance of ethics, he told King Pasenadi:

"If one regards oneself as dear
One should not yoke oneself to evil.
For happiness is not easily gained
By one who does a wrongful deed.
Both merits and evil,
That a mortal does right here
This is what is truly one's own
This is what follows one along
Like a shadow that never departs."

The Buddha went on to speak to the King about attachment to possessions and mistreating others, he said:

"Far more numerous in the world are those who obtain superior possessions and then become intoxicated and negligent and then mistreat others.
They do not realise they have gone too far.
Each person holds himself most dear.
Hence one who loves himself should not harm others."

In a battle, King Pasenadi had defeated King Ajatasattu and confiscated from his enemy everything he had but let King Ajatasattu go free with nothing but his life. The Sangha reported to the Buddha news of the battle. The Buddha commented that:

"Victory breeds arrogance and enmity
while the defeated suffer anguish and cannot sleep.
Those who live in peace and sleep easily
have abandoned victory and defeat."

After the Battle, the Buddha said:

"A man will go on plundering

So long as it serves his ends.
But when others plunder him
The plunderer is plundered.
The fool thinks fortune is on his side
So long as his evil does not ripen
But when the evil ripens
The fool incurs suffering.
The killer begets a killer
The abuser begets abuse
By the unfolding of karma
The plunderer is plundered."

The Buddha dismissed, out of hand, the view that the birth of a son mattered more than the birth of a daughter. A dejected King Pasenadi went to the Buddha and whispered to him that his wife, Queen Mallika, had given birth to a daughter and he felt "displeased." Despite the strongly held cultural view of preference of the birth of a son over a daughter, especially from powerful families, the Buddha told him simply and directly: *"A woman may turn out better than a man."*

The Buddha went on to tell the King that he had to set an example to his subjects. *"You should train yourself. 'I will be one with good friends, good companions and good comrades.' Your subjects will then think the same."* The Buddha knew the corruption among royalty, politicians, financiers, civil servants, religious leaders and the military easily provoked further corruption among the rest of the population.

Kind Pasenadi invited the Buddha to take a meal with him. The Buddha saw the King eating large measures of rice and curry. He told the King to go on a diet.

"When a man is always mindful
Knowing moderation in the food he eats

His ailments then diminish
He ages slowly, guarding his life."

The King took the Buddha's advice and in time became "quite slim." The King commented: "The Buddha showed compassion towards me in the regard to my present and future."

No wonder, the high priests of secular mindfulness keep a distance from the radical vision of the Buddha: he gave fearless feedback to the rich and powerful and had willingness to name and specify the greed, blame and delusion in their consciousness. For compassion to express, it requires true grit to specify the issues and the change required in behaviour.

The application of mindfulness and concentration works for the relief of suffering, employing the capacity to make critical judgements, wise discernment and the application of a polemic to open up a dialogue and accountability. This will not happen if practitioners identify with the view that mindfulness means looking into the present moment free from judgement. Compassion comprises of looking into the present moment, seeing and knowing any suffering that reveals it*self*, knowing the causes and conditions and seeing the way forward to resolve this. Compassion requires judgements to go forward.

The experience of being well established in the 'Now' offers a means to trigger an outpouring of compassion. It is also a sign of being on the path to a genuine awakening. Being in the here and now as a spiritual dogma has a ruinous impact on social and global life. Instead of spending so much time dwelling in the now, and the *self*'s involvement in the now, people might find more compassion in their being if they gave some thoughtful concerns to the long term future, the loss of resources, the destruction of environment and the remnants of a civilisation. What will be left for our children, grandchildren and future generations. Instead of refusing to think ahead, to reflect on causes/conditions and effects, we have become saddled with this foolish view that being in the now is an end in it*self*.

We are equally discouraged from turning our attention to the past. This shows another naïve, if not dangerous view. We turn our attention to the past to learn from the past.

- *What are the causes and conditions that led up to a painful situation?*
- *What was the sequence of events, whether personal or political, that generated problems, great and small?*
- *What shows the impact of the past on the present?*

The dismissal of past and future actively inhibits compassion. Reflection, meditation and insights into processes, into factors of contingency, into cause and effect, matter far more than being mindful in the moment without making judgements.

It could equally be said that the capacity to stand back from others, and to know separation, gives the opportunity to see clearly and comprehend the application of the Four Truths and act with compassion. The capacity to stand back from ones '*self*,' others and events shows the way to the release of compassion. If we have our hand too close to our eyes, we cannot see clearly the condition of the hand, the lines, the marks, and distinguish the various features. Separation of the hand from the eyes, the making of a distance, gives the opportunity for clear comprehension.

The experience of non-separation may contribute to a genuine sense of intimacy and concerns for others as we go through this process of birth, ageing, pain and death. Through our oneness experience, we feel we all share so much together. Such a view would profoundly influence our political, social and global perspectives. Oneness dissolves the notion of enemies, of "them," of the "other." We could no longer support the military interventions of the nation state.

The view of non-separation also has its shadow. It can inhibit our capacity to stand back and see clearly. If there is a tendency towards wishing to please others, to be passive, to say only what will be accepted, then the non-separate experience works against the clarity and freedom to express. Illusions can arise in separation and non-separation, since both sides of this duality remain contingent on the circumstances, especially with regard to the release of compassion.

Diet and Compassion

The Buddha strongly advocated love and compassion for all beings, not only human beings but also creatures in the air, on the ground, in the water and under the ground. Lay people in India supported wanderers, spiritual seekers, yogis, monks and nuns with a vegetarian diet. They did not offer cooked animals, birds or fish to eat. The Buddha insisted that dedicated practitioners *"train themselves to be pure in body, speech and mind, guard the senses, moderate in eating, mindful and vigilant."* (MN I 271-280). Only a few Buddhists today have chosen a vegetarian diet and even fewer still have adopted a vegan diet. Vegans and vegetarians do not eat animals, birds or fish, and vegans, in addition, do not consume dairy, eggs, or honey.

Motives and intentions influence the reasons to be vegan or vegetarian. While Buddhists generally speaking eat meat and fish, more and more voices in the Buddhist

205

traditions, whether Tibetan Mahayana, Theravada or Zen, advocate a major change in diet out of compassion for animals rather than for personal health reasons (even though a nutritious vegan or vegetarian diet contributes to personal health). A plant-based diet is crucial in protecting our delicate environment.

Some Buddhist meditation centres and monasteries in the West offer a vegetarian diet which contributes to encouraging Buddhists and others to become vegetarians, while other centres and monasteries serve meat and fish. Centres which provide a nutritious vegetarian diet often offer a further option to be vegan and will use soya milk instead of dairy milk. Only a small number of Dharma teachers and leaders are strict vegetarian or vegan in their daily life. There needs to be encouragement for Dharma teachers, centres and communities to advocate a vegan or vegetarian diet in daily life in order to reduce the suffering of farm animals. Important campaigns take place such as Dharma *Voice for Animals* –*www.Dharmavoicesforanimals.org* – to give voice to animals and their fate.

It is not easy for vegetarians to let go of dairy products i.e. milk, butter, yogurt and cheese. It is often as difficult a transition as going from a meat/fish diet to vegetarian. Renunciation directly contributes to feeding the world's hungry whether one is a vegetarian, vegan or primarily vegetarian or primarily vegan, by demanding plant-based food since this is grown much more efficiently than food from animals.

Ten Compassionate Reasons
to be Vegan

1.   *A plant based diet saves the lives of animals, birds and fish year in and year out. Farm animals and birds face the terror of slaughter at the abattoirs as they are lined up one behind the other, for execution. It is estimated that a person living to 75 years of age consumes around 6600 animals, birds and fish, including 2200 chickens.*

2.   *Antibiotics, growth hormones, and pesticides affect the cells of farm animals and those who eat them.*

3.   *Farm animals, such as sheep, cows and pigs, are generally calm and trusting creatures. Animals respond to love and can feel pain. They may have the mentality of babies and very young children. To produce a pound of beef, cattle consume 2500 gallons of water and crops that could feed humans. It takes 13 lbs of plant-based food to produce 1lb of animal flesh. The huge number of acres used to grow crops and other plant based food to feed animals could go to feed the world's hungry. 75% of topsoil has been depleted due to farm animals.*

4.   *The UN reports that the raping of rainforests for cattle grazing affects the climate. Rainforest destruction brings about more greenhouse gases that affect the climate than all transport, air, land and water.*

5.   *The varieties of forests provide food and medicine for people worldwide. Greenhouse gases release methane, ammonia, and nitrous oxide, and carbon dioxide into the atmosphere through burning of wood, gas, oil and coal. Pollution affects land, water, air and forests, as well as the health of people and animals.*

6.   Livestock farms have become factories known as Concentrated Animal Feeding Operations (CAFO). Living in controlled, tight, intensely overcrowded environments, these animals live a hellish life. They also produce huge amounts of urine and excrement waste polluting land, water tables and rivers.

7.   Millions of calves and male chicks are slaughtered as waste to ensure milk and egg production.

8.   The livestock industry is responsible for 18% of global greenhouse gas emissions. The transport sector is responsible for 13.5% of global emissions planes, cars, trucks, and trains.

9.   The 'typical' US diet generates the equivalent of nearly 1.5 tonnes more carbon dioxide per person per year than a vegan diet.

10.   It is far more sustainable to eat plant foods than animals in order to feed the rapidly growing world population of seven billion plus people, especially as available land decreases. Through a vegan diet, or a virtually vegan diet, our eco footprint treads lightly on the earth.

Some vegans apply strict disciplines to diet and dress to support animals' welfare and biodiversity. They refuse to eat eggs, honey, wear leather, (leather shoes or leather belt) and do not wear wool and silk. They show the lay equivalent of the Buddhist monks' Rules of Discipline (*Vinaya*).

The meat industry campaigns to get people to eat animals with claims that meat provides the necessary protein, even though a plant-based diet can fully satisfy protein requirement see www.pcrm.org. Much protein is lost in the cooking of meat. People have made the transition from meat and fish to becoming fully committed vegans with more than enough protein coming from quinoa, beans, lentils, nuts, tofu and tempeh.

Some consider personal health reasons for becoming vegan:

- *On average, a vegan weighs 20 lbs less than a meat eater and there is therefore less strain and pressure on every part of the body.*
- *A vegan does not consume cholesterol and saturated animal fat in meat, eggs and dairy products, giving protection to the heart, vital organs and arteries.*
- *A vegan diet, rich in vitamins, antioxidants and fibre, decreases the chances of suffering from diseases such as diabetes, heart disease, stroke and certain cancers. Mindfulness of the amount of sugar, salt and fat consumed is necessary for every kind of diet.*

While food from local farms saves on transportation costs, we can find wonderful vegan meals world-wide. Exceptionally tasty, plant based diets include:

- *green and red curries with coconut milk from Thailand,*
- *hummus and falafels from the Middle East,*
- *Mexican beans and tortillas,*
- *pasta, vegetables with herbs from Italy,*
- *rice, curry and lentils from India,*
- *tofu and stir fry from China/Japan.*

Readers can check out these websites for excellent recipes.

- http://dharmavoicesforanimals.org
- www.vegnews.com
- http://www.vrg.org/recipes

Vegan food is often quick and easy to prepare with instructions from cookbooks, recipes from the internet line and cooking videos on YouTube.

We may view acts of renunciation, such as stopping eating creatures with a face, as an austere approach to daily life, whereas such changes can contribute to opening up our world and our senses. The act of renunciation becomes an expression of compassion.

The Media and Compassion

News reports on television, the radio and newspapers specialise in reporting suffering (the First Noble Truth) . There is little sustained investigation into the causes/conditions of suffering or, the resolution of suffering. Articles that give analysis to such suffering rarely touch upon the emotional/psychological elements in the human behaviour of politicians, bankers, terrorists or criminals. Newspapers often give a slanted report based on the underlying ideology of the owner of the news organisation, or attempt to offer a balanced view. The balanced view tends to uphold the status quo.

We need news reporting that offers more than the so-called facts (of suffering) but also includes insights into the depth and breadth of psychological influences that generate much of the suffering. Peace and reconciliation ministers need to replace defence ministers in national governments. Weapons of mass destruction and weapons of life destruction need to be replaced with tools of mass construction and tools of life construction to resolve human conflicts.

No matter how fast the flow of information from the source of conflict to our screens and publications, we still live in the dark ages in terms of the exploration of the Truth of the contingency factors for suffering and letting go of them.

Government ministers, lawmakers, the judiciary, university research and political analysts rarely consider the psychological dynamic of those who make war and support violence from air, land or sea. Have our leaders developed a Pathological mental illness (disguised as rational decision making and emotionless speeches) when they use weaponry from land, sea and air for the killing and maiming of men, women and children, assassinations, summary arrests and psychological/physical torture? Absence of emotional engagement and the total reliance of logic, of cold rationalisations, to employ the military to inflict suffering, does not show sanity but a deeply flawed, deeply fragmented human being whose personality in office has cut off, or dried up all feelings, emotions and concerns for the "other." This is a form of psychological/emotional madness in the lives of men and women in power.

We have the right to ask basic questions even if the questions sound offensive:

- *Is the world a lunatic asylum run by the patients?*
- *Are our leaders mad?*
- *Do they need intensive psychological counselling/meditation retreats and a wise Sangha?*
- *Should our leaders, who support the destruction of life and habitats, be taken into care in habitats where they can receive support to work on themselves?*
- *Are they capable of showing compassion to one and all without exception?*

Madness expresses as the lack of unconditional empathy, an unfeeling relationship to adults and children who live and think in a different way. An emotionally well-adjusted human being lives with compassion extending in all directions without limits. We have reason to suspect that the mentally ill rule our lives. It is an act of compassion to find skilful ways to stop our leaders and their military/corporate backers from inflicting suffering on armies, organisations and civilians anywhere in the world.

The Viewer of Suffering and Compassion

We have to ask ourselves about the impact of televised suffering on our screens, the grim photographs in the media and the heart-breaking details of reports in the press in general on all manner of human, animal, environmental issues. It would appear that the viewing of suffering through the media impacts in very unsatisfactory ways on far too many people. Some feel inspired to act, to work to make a real change to reduce or end the suffering they see in the media. The great majority have questions to ask:

1. *Is there a numbing of the emotional capacity to respond to the suffering reported daily in our media?*

2. *Is the viewing of suffering a form of voyeurism where we sit and watch, sit and listen, sit and read about the hell in people's lives, and yet not act?*

3. *Do we experience momentary pity at the plight of others, devoid of compassion that generate action distinct from compassion.*

4. *Have we seen/heard/read so many reports of suffering that we are left with a general sense of apathy?*

5. *Do we feel helpless after seeing the news? 'What can I do? What can one individual do in the face of these powerful people?'*

6. *Do we experience so called compassion fatigue - not only the compassion fatigue experienced by those who work tirelessly for others and neglect or lack the skills for regular renewal. There is also the fatigue at seeing and hearing so many reports of suffering that we cannot then find the energy to initiate or join others to work in a field of compassion.*

7. *Have we become desensitised to the suffering of people both on a large and small scale?*

8. *Have our hearts become cold when aid organisations and charities put out desperate appeals for help to end a crisis?*

9. *Do we share the old Latin maxim: pereat mundus, dum ego salvus sium - May the world perish, provided I am safe?*

People can find themselves utterly unable to respond to information and stories about suffering. They feel helpless and powerless. They do not know what to do. Donating money always helps. It is the quickest and easiest response. You put your hand in your pocket and take out your credit card, cheque book, wallet or purse and give money. It takes barely a couple of minutes.

The Buddha detailed the two psychological forces that inhibit wisdom and compassion. The first is the desire for one's own well-being/pleasure/comfort above all else. The second force is negativity, namely the desire to blame others and support infliction of pain upon others.

Our helplessness, numbness and compassion fatigue ensure the status quo cripples our capacity to act for the welfare of others, near and far. The exploration of the second Noble Truth of inquiry into the causes and conditions for suffering includes exploring the consequences of violence, and the psychological, social and ideological structures that perpetuate violence including despair, rejection of the other, poverty, violence in movies, war games, boxing, state executions, abattoirs, animal suffering, war heroes and more.

Politicians and their defenders tell us that the "other" has inflicted unspeakable and obscene violence upon us, and we plan to inflict more of the same. They say that we have to act to stop them from doing it again and we must inflict suffering on them to stop them. The "others" have been told that we have inflicted unspeakable and obscene violence upon them, and they plan to inflict more of the same upon us to stop us - to get us off their land, out of their country.

We can walk on the Earth with dignity and establish a way of being that has moved far beyond the desire for retribution, punishment and other desperate measures. We have the capacity to act and see things differently from our leaders who can lord their destructive will over people's lives.

The act of compassion, the act of wise engagement, expresses sanity, a noble constitution that far outranks in its significance any identification with the nation state whether tied to secular or religious beliefs or both.

In the dedication to compassion, it may be that, at times, we must endure the outbursts of people of violence who wish to stifle our voices and marginalise our actions.

We can stay true to openness, love and integrity. We can go far beyond the limits of our shrivelled little *self* that disappears down the rabbit hole at the first sign of a threat.

With compassion, we give support to those who suffer.

May all beings live with love
May al beings live with compassion
May all beings live with wisdom

Outline of Buddha's Discourses (Suttas)

MN - Middle Length Discourses of the Buddha (Pali: Majjhima Nikaya)
DN - Longer Discourses of the Buddha (Digha Nikaya)
SN - Connected Discourses of the Buddha (Samyutta Nikaya)
AN - Numerical Discourses of the Buddha
Sn - Sutta Nipata
Dh - Dhammapada
It - Itivuttaka
Ud - Udana

Number besides letters of discourse indicates the discourse. For example MN 29 *refers to discourse number 29 in Middle Length Discourses.*

The Suttas are grouped into various collections.

1. **The Middle Length Discourses of the Buddha (MD)** translated by Bhikkhu Bodhi from Majjhima Nikaya. Wisdom Publications, Massachusetts in 1995.

2. **The Long Discourses of the Buddha (DN)** translated by Maurice Walshe from the Digha Nikaya Wisdom Publications, 361 Newbury Street, Boston, Massachusetts 02115, U.S.A. in 1995.

3. **The Book of the Gradual Discourses (AN)** translated by E.M. Hare from the Anguttara-Nikaya. 5 volumes approximately 1400 pages published by Pali Text Society and Unwin Brothers Limited, The Gresham Press, Old Woking, Surrey in 1978.

4. **The Connected Discourses of the Buddha (SN)** translated by Bhikkhu Bodhi from the Samyutta-Nikaya, approximately 2174 pages publication date, November 2000. By Wisdom Publications, Boston, Massachusetts, Pali Text Society, London in 1980.

5. **The Sutta-Nipata** (Sn) translated by H. Saddhatissa from Samyutta-Nikaya. 135 pages published by Curzon Press Limited, 42 Gray's Inn Road, London WC1 in 1985.

6. **The Dhammapada** (Dp)(423 verses) translated by Acharya Buddharakkhita, introduction by Bhikkhu Bodhi the Buddhist Publication Society, Kandy, Sri Lanka.

7. **The Udana and The Itivuttaka,**(Ud,It) translated by John D. Ireland, Buddhist Publication Society, Kandy Sri Lanka.

Books by Christopher Titmuss

Spirit for Change
Freedom of the Spirit
Fire Dance and Other Poems
The Profound and The Profane
The Green Buddha
Light on Enlightenment
The Power of Meditation
The Little Box of Inner Calm
An Awakened Life
The Buddha's Book of Daily Meditations
Buddhist Wisdom for Daily Living
Transforming Our Terror
Sons and Daughters of The Buddha
Mindfulness for Everyday Living
Mindfulness Training Course
Poems from the Edge
Meditation Healing

Books to be published. 2015-2016

The Explicit Buddha
The Inquiring Buddha
The Political Buddha
The Buddha in the West

Websites

www.insightmeditation.org
www.mindfulnesstrainingcourse.org
www.DharmaEnquiry.org
www.dharmayatra.org
www.bodhgayaretreats.org
www.christophertitmuss.org

MAY ALL BEINGS LIVE WITH LOVE
MAY ALL BEINGS LIVE WITH INSIGHT
MAY ALL BEINGS LIVE AN AWAKENED LIFE